6/25

Alaska As It Used To Was

John Thompson

Copyright © 2002 by John Thompson

All rights reserved. No part of this book shall be reproduced or transmitted in any form or by any means, electronic, mechanical, magnetic, photographic including photocopying, recording or by any information storage and retrieval system, without prior written permission of the publisher. No patent liability is assumed with respect to the use of the information contained herein. Although every precaution has been taken in the preparation of this book, the publisher and author assume no responsibility for errors or omissions. Neither is any liability assumed for damages resulting from the use of the information contained herein.

ISBN 0-7414-1052-4

Published by:

INFINITY
PUBLISHING.COM

519 West Lancaster Avenue
Haverford, PA 19041-1413
Info@buybooksontheweb.com
www.buybooksontheweb.com
Toll-free (877) BUY BOOK
Local Phone (610) 520-2500
Fax (610) 519-0261

Printed in the United States of America

Printed on Recycled Paper

Published March, 2002

Table of Contents

HOP ABOARD, WE'RE HEADIN' FOR ALASKA ... 1
CHANGE, A NEW EXPERIENCE ... 4
CATCH A CAN ... 7
CRAIG ... 11
PLEASE STAY ... 17
WORK APLENTY ... 19
TIME AND TIDE ... 24
NO SEE UM ... 28
SCAT CAT ... 32
GRATITUDITY PLUS ... 34
A WHALE BALLET ... 39
A DAMSEL IN DISTRESS ... 42
QUEENIE ... 45
ALASKA THE BEAUTIFUL ... 50
DAMMIT ... 55
SPRING MEANS SALMON ... 59
DAMMIT AGAIN ... 65
G'BYE CRAIG - - - HELLO KLAWOCK ... 68
SOCIAL STATUS ... 70
FOOD - - APLENTY ... 74
CLAMMING – BUT DOING IT RIGHT ... 76
A GENUINE TASTE OF BUCK FEVER ... 81

DAHKEENOO-EASTER	84
THE FAMILY TREE	92
NAHSUK- - WOLF ISLAND	96
LOVE IN BLOOM	101
BEARLY MISSED	105
THE LEGEND OF KUSH DA KAH	107
THE GEESE HUNTER	114
EXOTIC FOOD	118
A NEAR TRAGEDY!	123
ALL THAT GLITTERS	129
GAMBOLING THROUGH THE MUSKEGS	134
A FISH GAVE ME THE BIRD	138
A TYPICAL CANNING SEASON	142
LIVERING IT UP	145
A LEGEND IN HIMSELF	149
INTENSE WAS THE BATTLE	153
FUN FISHING OR DISASTER	157
HEY, ANYBODY GOT A BATTERY	160
INDIAN FOOD GOOD	162
BEARLY MADE IT	167
YA WANNA PLAY TUG-A-WAR	170
PAT MY BACK - - I'LL PAT YOURS	176
DUK DUUK – THE NORTH WIND	181
LEGEND OF THE EAST WIND	185
A DOUBLE TRAGEDY	187
SAVED BY THE BIRD	191

INTRODUCTION

"Alaska, As It Used To Was," is exciting and definitely a must. You will be unable to simply lay it aside, once you've begun reading it.

Every page offers insight into a lifestyle known only to those who ventured North to participate in this unique way of life.

Acknowledgement

I'm dedicating this book to my four sons Gregory Jon, Gerry Bruce, Jay Carl, and Jeffrey Charles, so that they may know a side of me they did not know.

HOP ABOARD, WE'RE HEADIN' FOR ALASKA

It all started way back in 1947 where I was employed in Portland, Oregon at a small shop with my working partner Cal Dawson. We heard that our shop was nearing the end of its latest contract, with no new work in sight—a definite sign that there would be a layoff in the near future.

Cal happened to have relatives residing in Alaska at this particular time, who had been encouraging him to come on up North and join them. They further enticed him into doing so by announcing that work was available, then also offered him a house to use, rent free, should he decide to take them up on their offer. Needless to say, shortly thereafter Cal and his wife Wanda, were on their way North to a small town in Southeast Alaska, named Craig. Craig is located approximately 75 miles West of Ketchikan on the Prince of Wales group of Islands. Cal left with the promise that he would keep me informed about his impression of Craig, and also if work was available for me as well.

Less than a week had transpired when I received word from Cal that Alaska was outstandingly beautiful, besides the fact that opportunity beckoned and work was plentiful. Wow! In addition to that we were also offered a place to stay, rent free, for as long as we wished should we decide to come North. My wife and I were rather reluctant to commit to anything permanent, so instead opted to do nothing more than just visit for a couple of weeks. After all, we reasoned, didn't we have two weeks severance pay in our jeans? Weren't we entitled to a vacation. So after such rational and clever thinking, we prepared to venture North. Won't you please join us?

Those of you who have never flown before will be experiencing the same feelings and excitement as my wife and I as we leave the security of our home in Portland to begin our trip North. We shall endeavor to take you along with us, at least mentally if not physically. As we approach the plane for boarding you will no doubt be in awe that this monstrous winged apartment house can actually lift itself from the ground. You will also be amazed that this huge aircraft is capable of climbing skywards so rapidly that cars and buildings below appear as almost indiscernible objects in a matter of seconds.

Upon reaching an altitude in the vicinity of 25,000 to 30,000 feet, the huge craft will soon level off, affording you a breathtaking view of the landscape below. What a magnificent sight when viewed from the air. The whole scenario ever changing, as though viewing through a giant kaleidoscope, only much more defined. Now that we are genuinely committed into heading North, our first stop shall be Seattle, Washington, where we will stay overnight. The following morning, bright and early, we are airborne once more. Very soon after takeoff you will observe the Olympic range of mountains slithering by beneath us, sparkling and glistening in their mantle of new fallen snow.

It is the month of February, and it is still early in the morning. What luck, because you may now witness the sun eagerly at work creating awesome patterns in highlighting the peaks of mountains, while at the same time it is equally as busy casting contrasting black shadows in their deep canyons and crevices. What magnificence! The thought must surely be entering your mind, "Wow, it's as though Picasso is sitting beside me fabricating those beautiful black and whites for which he is so singulariy renowned." Your excitement will mount even higher when you realize that, as the tail of this big 'ol DC 10 leaves the Olympic range in it's wake, you are quite possibly flying over some part of Alaska. A more positive likelihood, that this may be true, has already been confirmed as greater amounts of snow can be seen covering the surrounding mountains. In addition to that, the scenery is becoming more and more blotted from view as more and more clouds form around the aircraft.

Now while you are wondering where in the world you are at this particular point in time, the seat belt sign goes, "Ding," followed by an announcement over the plane's speaker system. "Ladies and Gentlemen, we will be landing at Annette Island shortly. May I remind you, be sure your seat belt is securely fastened, etc., etc." Now you mustn't become too overly excited because you have not quite reached your destination at this moment. However, I guarantee that Annette Island will prove to be an unexpected adventure in itself.

CHANGE, A NEW EXPERIENCE

Okay folks! Brace yourselves for entering into a lifestyle completely opposite from that to which you are accustomed. In the event that you're not naturally endowed with the ability to accept a radical change in your normal day-to-day routine, then sorry. You'll probably never make it in this vast and unique North Country.

Hang on! Our giant craft is now in the act of touching down. Permit me to introduce you to Annette Island, home to the Tsimpsian Indians of Massett, B.C. (British Columbia). From here it is but a short hop North to Ketchikan. However, I'm afraid you'll discover that short hops here in the North Country entail much more effort than merely jumping into a nice shiny automobile. In fact, during the 1950's there were relatively very few cars in the whole of Alaska. Those that were here occupied space in only the larger towns, such as Juneau, Alaska's capitol, Ketchikan, Anchorage, and maybe Fairbanks.

You are about to discover that Annette Island is inhabited solely by Tsimpsian Indians, who live in a village named Metlakatla, fifteen miles or so to the South of the airport. Because of their proximity to the airport the villagers are employed by the airlines to service the large planes that land here before they continue northward, bound for Anchorage and Fairbanks. Therefore, whatever personal services you may derive during your stay on the island, shall come from these Tsimpsian Indians who, incidentally, are not prone to pampering outsiders.

At long last we are finally on the ground, the plane has come to a complete stop, and we are being disgorged from the plane into a couple of decrepit old busses that most assuredly lacked a shiny and lustrous paint job. The road we are traversing is unpaved, which unfortunately has encouraged the busses to rattle and shake to the best of their ability, as though initiating us into our first dramatic taste of change.

From this point our busses continue with their initiation ceremonies for a distance of several agonizing miles. Following this jostling ride we shall be unceremoniously discharged from the heavily panting busses, into an ancient quonset hut used by the military during World War II. Immediately thereafter, we find ourselves being introduced onto a line of wooden benches circumventing the interior of the "terminal?" The benches are rock hard and they shall become even harder as we resign ourselves to await the arrival of an Albatross, supposedly within the hour.

An irate passenger sharing the bench just a few seats to our right vented his anger at the delay by bellering, "Hey, what the Hell's this about some damn bird holdin us up?" "Whoa, hold it a minute there, fella! Lets get this straight. For your information an Albatross in this instance is not a bird as you might assume from the name, but rather than that, is actually a vintage, twin-engined seaplane. Not only was it designed for landing in the water, it was also equipped with wheels which permitted it to land on asphalt runways as well."

Hence, the reason for the delay at Annette was due to the fact that there was no other plane available at the present time, which offered a combination of this magnitude. So sit we must wait, without even a smidgen of preparation H mind you, until the Albatross arrives from Sitka to transport us into Ketchikan where we would be reassigned to Ellis Airlines. Ellis Air employed an amphibious operation out of Ketchikan. Their task was to distribute those passengers who arrived from stateside, onward to their destinations in S. E.

Alaska. Which included Juneau, Wrangell, Petersburg, Sitka, or any one of a number of small villages having no landing strips other than water. Craig was also on the list, our final destination.

CATCH A CAN

C'mon gang, take off time at last, It's goodbye to Annette, and onward to Ketchikan. Did I not tell you Annette would be an experience in itself?

Catch a can, what an appropriate name for the flying machine that just arrived at Annette to transport us into Ketchikan where we shall be reassigned to Ellis Airline for our trip to Craig.

It was such a relief for all to realize that we had not been completely forgotten. You know, any of you that have had the opportunity to witness an Albatross take flight from a body of water will readily associate that bird, with this bird. The Albatross eagerly demonstrated how accurately it could live up to it's name as it began to rattle and shake in making a strenuous effort to become airborne with visibility at ground zero, no less.

It was easy to determine that it was raining because water could be seen dripping down on a number of the passengers. At the same time our male steward was busily engaged in swiping at the drips with a roll of paper towels, while apologizing to each of the passengers for their discomfort. In view of the shaking, rattling, and dripping, my wife leaned over against me, whispering, "We surely must be going to make it, certainly the pilot doesn't want to die!"

She was almost right, but with one more heart stopper. No one had bothered to inform her that we were in a seaplane combo, so as we prepared to land in the water she became unglued. She grasped my arm so tightly she nearly drew blood as she gasped, "What in the world is he doing? My gawd, we're going to hit the water."

Unfortunately, there was no time for an explanation. The Albatross literally plopped down into the water, half submerging, then bobbing back to the surface with the propellers going plap, plap, plap as they batted the water aside. Poor lady! She reluctantly regained her composure as she observed her fellow passengers taking this, all in stride---so settled down to sightseeing as before. After having taxied on the water up to the Ellis float, we were obliged to spend several hours transferring baggage and verifying our tickets, but were also advised that we would be detained, awaiting a goose. (good chance for a bit of ribaldry there)

However, having to wait once again proved to be very rewarding as we spent our time observing an unusual amount of activity directly before our eyes in Revilligigido channel, so called since Ketchikan is located on Revilligigido Island. The harbor was alive with a swarm of small float-planes busily creating a symphony of sound in their comings and goings. Resembling a flock of birds, they were landing and taking off up and down the harbor in what appeared to us to be a very helter-skelter manner, with no regard whatsoever as to flight patterns or order of any kind.

We formed our own opinion that they were without a doubt, misplaced New York cabbies in a strange environment. Do not fool yourselves on this point. These pilots know exactly what they are doing. Bush pilots, as they are called up here, are the unsung heroes of the North Country.

Their willingness to fly under adverse weather conditions, is a challenge they accept as a part of their every day lives. They are your search and rescue teams. They are the part of Alaska that used to was, the ones who made it what it is today. Alaska would likely have not survived at all were it not for these dedicated men. The bush pilot delivers the mail to the numerous villages scattered throughout the territory.

They accept the risk involved in flying heavy pieces of equipment to logging and mining camps. Their cargo may at times be as variable as a box of iced down fish, a deceased person, or a team of sled dogs for the Iditarod competition as far North as Nome.

So it's back to the harbor where our attention is now drawn to a deep rumbling sound. Sort of like tooma, tooma, tooma, tooma. Lo and behold, a huge tug pokes its nose into the picture, with an enormous log raft in tow, and of all things, its headin right up the center of the channel. What we are hearing is the tug's huge diesel engines producing this booming sound, during its approach into Ketchikans front yard, so to speak. I told you, you'd see a lot of things you never expected to see on this trip, didn't I?

Talk about fun! The tug was towing a raft twice as long as any football field, right smack dab up the center of the Revilligigido channel, forcing the swarm of small planes to take evasive action in their taking off and landing patterns. The pilots proved to be quite adept in veering either right or left, or skimming over the raft in order to land safely. When taking off, they took advantage of the bumpy water created by the tow, affording themselves a much faster lift off.

Things have quieted down a little now, since the tug has finally tugged its way clear of the harbor. Things have gone back to that same activity which grabbed our attention in the first place, and we are again on hold, waiting for our goose. At this point in time we are all of one mind, thinking, "Hey, maybe someone's giving us the bird," when, can you believe this? A goose lights upon the water and taxies up to the Ellis float.

A friendly fella from Alaska standing on the float beside us, finally put an end to, "The dilemma of the birds." He volunteered that the Grumman Aircraft Corporation had designed a series of aircraft, each one suited to the needs of the Alaska trade. As a token of appreciation for the contracts, the company elected to name the newly purchased aircraft after the waterfowl most common to the area. Thus the Widgeon, the Goose, and the Mallard were born for the Alaska trade. It was purely coincidental that the blankety blank Albatross happened to bear a name relative to the others because it was not part of the modernization plan in any way shape or form. The old bucket of bolts most assuredly must have been left over from the World War II era.

CRAIG

It is time! However exciting Ketchikan has proven to be, our plane which is bound for the West Coast has finally arrived and we are now boarding---destination Craig. The plane is a twin-engined Grumman Goose, totally amphibious. At this point I turned to my wife to emphasize the fact that amphibious means, "This is a seaplane," so it will definitely land in the water. The plane has a displacement for seven passengers with one seat located beside the pilot. This is where I am positioned for the flight to Craig.

Fortunately for all concerned the pilot was very talkative and informative during the flight. We were advised that our destination would be approximately seventy-five miles West of Ketchikan on the Prince of Wales group of Islands. Furthermore, we would be flying a little bit South through Chomley Straits, since Haidaburg would be our first stop. Uh huh, I nodded, like oh sure, I know what way is South.

In a matter of minutes soon after crossing a fairly large body of water, we were able to spot land up ahead. Again the pilot volunteered that we had just crossed Dixon Entrance, the main channel for sea-going vessels on their way to various inland ports throughout the territory. Flying in these smaller planes was contrary to flying stateside due to the fact that everywhere we flew we were right down low, barely tree top high. Flying this low was quite advantageous in one respect since it afforded us a birds-eye view of the surrounding countryside. However, I 'm certain the pilot was well aware of the number of times I raised my feet for fear of getting my damn heels busted. He said nothing, but I caught him out of the corner of my eye, grinning like a horse eating thistles, over the antics of the Cheechako riding shotgun for him.

As a precautionary gesture I was forewarned that as soon as we had crossed Chomley we would be flying through a pass, then when upon reaching the opposite end of the pass, Haidaburg should appear on our right. Entering the pass had a very sobering affect on me, especially as I witnessed the wing tips of our plane just barely clearing the trees on each side of us as we entered this vee between two mountains. One thing always seems to compensate for another up here in the North Country. At the same time that we were skimming past the trees I was inadvertently rewarded in spotting a number of very rare bald headed Eagles resting on a couple of old snags right beside the plane as we roared by. Damndumbbirds. They didn't even budge. It was probably because my mouth flew open in amazement that our informer informed us, matter of factly, "They're used to seeing us. We fly through here almost every day."

By this time I'm wising up fast and I've condescended to put my complete trust in our sky jockey. Therefore, I have really settled back to relax and enjoy these numerous and unfamiliar happenings. Then in an effort to test my undeclared trust in him, the pilot suddenly nosed the plane downward so that we might better observe a pod of whales traversing the channel directly below us. Two thrills! A chill from taking the dive. A thrill for actually having seen some whales.

Immediately following the whale incident, I find myself being exposed to yet another test of faith in our pilot's abilities. A mountain suddenly reared up directly in our path. So what's to worry? That little old Grumman Goose simply climbed right up the face of that big o'l hill, brrrr. The pilot assured me there was nothing to be concerned about, since these planes are equipped with very powerful motors. "In fact," he confided in me, "They are able to fly on only one motor should it become necessary." "Thank you, but no thanks," I confided right back.

As we reached the top of the mountain the ground beneath us immediately disappeared and we found ourselves suspended some 1500 feet in the air, when the plane decided to rectify this by quickly dropping a hundred feet or so. The pilot, through some sixth sense of his own, or perhaps it was the fact that my eyes bugged out far enough to cover some part of his instrument panel, came to the conclusion that I had become a little unnerved over this heart stopping incident. So once again, ho hum! "These drops are quite common. You see there are thermals on this side of the peak but when we reach the opposite side there are none. So naturally the plane drops a little until we pick up the thermals again." (Little) I wondered if the Alaskan dictionary defined little in the same tenor that I felt at the time.

After climbing then dropping with no thermals, while inadvertently swallowing my innards several more times, we literally dove downward between two perpendicular cliffs then leveled out like a duck making ready to land. We then splashed down into the water, we half submerged, we popped to the surface, the props sang plap, plap, plap, the pilot shouted, "Haidaburg!" and everyone took a deep breath. The pilot directed his remark to me, declaring, "We'll be taking off for Craig soon as I dump the mail and a couple of passengers."

Shortly thereafter we took off once again, fairly skimming the water then rising only enough to barely clear the tree tops as we passed over a few small islands. Now laying on her side, our Grumman Goose zoomed around some tall crags, dropped down quickly, when up popped Craig as we landed with a splash, sank a little, bobbed, the props sang plap,plap. Woosh! We then taxied into the Ellis Air float in Craig, Alaska. Journey's end.

Ya'all think that's something. You must remember. I promised you new experiences and adventure. So hang tight friends, there's lots more to come. At times I write in the singular. That is not my intention. In all phases of this voyage to Alaska you are all inclusive, so step forward and walk in my shoes with me..

As we disembarked from the plane, thank goodness our friend Cal was there to receive us. We were unaware prior to our arrival in Craig that Cal was in fact the agent in charge of the Ellis Air terminal here. He had been granted that position shortly after his arrival in town. Small wonder his letter confirmed that work was plentiful and opportunity beckoned.

New people arriving always created a stir in this small town of 150 inhabitants, so the plane we arrived on carrying the mail, created something of a social event. Due to common practice a good percentage of the townsfolk usually gathered round the float in anticipation for receiving their mail and packages, but mainly to chit chat with one another. Of course the rumor that Cal had people coming in from stateside had no bearing on the fact that the mayor, several store owners, and a couple of Moose members as well as a number of local residents had converged on the float this particular day. Introductions were in order as Cal introduced his guests to all of those who had come forth to welcome us.

We were overwhelmed by the apparent friendliness and warmness shown by all those we met, as we received invite after invite to drop by anytime for a cup of coffee and a visit. In fact, the whole rest of the day was shot due to our meeting and yapping with people as we headed for Cal's house.

Oh, oh, our luggage. Damn, I'd completely forgotten about our luggage still sitting down there on the float. Several hours had gone by since our arrival, so I was near to pushing the panic button when we heard a loud knocking at Cal's door. There stood a big Indian with our luggage piled high upon a hand truck. All he said was, "I know you are the ones, the new people here. I know this suitcases are yours, and I know you are going to stay to this house, so I bring them here." We were completely flabbergasted, but nevertheless thanked him profusely, then offered him money for his services. He flat out refused to accept it as he squared his shoulders, then proudly announced, "We help each other." Cal then introduced me to Billy Chuck, a full-fledged Thlinget Indian, adding that he was a jewel of a fellow and a friend to all. We were completely taken aback as all these things, honesty, friendliness and goodwill were being extended to us, and we weren't even Craig-ites, so to speak. Quite naturally, we were very impressed.

The following day we were invited to take a tour of the town, which consisted of about 155 inhabitants, most of who were white, but with a few Thlinget families residing here as well. The town is built on an Island having but one single-laned unpaved street, playing host to probably no more than eight buildings occupying space along its length which encompassed something like a quarter of a mile in it's entirety. Once again we were subjected to a round of introductions as we meandered through the town. One Mrs.Troy occupied the commissioner's office at the West end of town, followed by Florence Cogo's liquor store. Facing the street was J.L. Lucier's grocery and hardware store, while directly opposite was Charles Jones grocery. We then crossed the street to Ma Abel's ice cream shop, crossed back again to discover Joe Otto and Anna Dye's combination restaurant and bar, then recrossed another time in order to come upon Margaret and Jessie Thompson's bar and liquor store. By the by, I must mention Craig did have a post office, a Union oil dock and a Standard oil dock. That's all there was to the town of Craig.

There was a road leading out of town toward the South which led to what was called the cove and this is where the city float was located, offering a sheltered port for the fleet of smaller boats, (mainly trollers and small runabouts.) Located at the cove was also a combination machine shop and grocery store owned by the Demmert family, the U. S. Forest Service headquarters, and finally the highly regarded Moose Lodge.

We were advised that if it were not for the Moose Lodge, the town would prove to be quite listless. The Moose members were the nucleus of activity in Craig, taking on the task of caring for the elderly, sponsoring charity balls, organizing special events, which included parades, Halloween parties, ball games and Easter egg hunts for the kids. They also initiated Thanksgiving Day and Christmas Eve parties. You name it, the Moose did it all!.

PLEASE STAY

During the time we spent visiting in Craig the townsfolk were making plans, very effective plans might I add, to make sure we would remain in Craig and not leave after our two weeks vacation was over, as we had planned. We were becoming nicely acquainted with a fair percentage of the residents by this time and discovered that they had all gotten their heads together, working on us.

One afternoon, Norma Anderson, a store manager's wife, accosted my wife and I as we were strolling along on the board walkway traversing the town. "John, I would like to show you something." So saying, she led us towards a small cabin overlooking the bay. "No one has been living here. If by any chance you would consider not leaving but decide to stay," she continued, "The owner of this cabin has offered you the cabin rent free, for nothing more than your cleaning it and making it livable."

Soon after, as my wife and I were being shown the interior of the place, some of the locals, as if by chance, happened by to offer us some furniture, another volunteered a bed. One couple willed that we accept some bedding and blankets they'd had stored for years and years. Oh sure, like no one has use for blankets in Iciclesville. It escalated like wild fire from this point on. Some offered to bring paint, others would hang curtains. The ladies from town assured us we certainly wouldn't have to worry about cleaning and such, they'd do that while their menfolk painted. As if by appointment, in less than an hour's time there were at least a dozen of the townspeople urging us to stay--- all of them begging to help us get set up. Never in the world had we experienced genuine hospitality such as this. We were completely taken by storm.

After having revisited the cabin once more and after having discussed how seemingly sincere everyone had been in wanting us to remain in Craig, we decided to give it a try.

Party time, Alaska style!

Upon hearing that we had agreed to go for it, that very same evening mind you, people showed up armed with paint brushes and paint. One of the smarter ones brought in a case of beer. Boy oh boy, did the paint ever flow! A knock on the door revealed another well wisher packing an armful of curtains. It grew into a pretty good party when no one had to knock anymore, they just piled in with pots and pans and dishes and silverware. Yikes! We're being attacked by a colony of ants. On and on it went until that time when the paint was used up and the beer was gone, so was the painting done, with the cabin completely refurbished and ready for occupancy. I swear, we had as cute and clean a place as any on the Island, all like magic. The Alaska Fairy had waved her magic wand and we were hooked.

Late that night, everyone shook our hands and congratulated us on our decision to stay. They then quietly departed just a few at a time until mystically, my wife and I found ourselves standing alone in our snug little cabin with a fire already lit in the heating stove, sending forth it's warm glow. However, nothing will compare to the warm glow we were feeling for these wonderfully hospitable people in the town of Craig.

WORK APLENTY

After awakening the morning following our shivaree, I found myself bemoaning the situation I had gotten myself into. I had some seriously, negative thoughts racing through my rabid ape mind, like Holy geehosifatz what have I done? I was making awfully good money working as a welder while I was living in Portland. Now I find myself committed into living in a tiny little town with nary a sign of industrial activity whatsoever. Where in the world was I going to get a job? My anxiety quivers were alleviated almost within the hour as one Bailey Sandifer stopped by for a cup of coffee and a chat. The Alaska Fairy apparently was still waving that magic wand.

Bailey was the local magistrate and he had come over to offer me work.

I would like to remind you once more that these ongoing series of events I'm writing about, actually occurred before Alaska became a state in 1959. Territorial jurisdiction during the period before Alaska declared statehood befell the U.S.Commissioner's office, and the Alaska Territorial Police Department. For minor and scattered infractions of the law, a magistrate was appointed to uphold law and order in some of the outlying districts.

As I was saying. Bailey, the local magistrate had come over to offer me work. May I hold up right here, for a moment. I'm positive I unwittingly misspelled the word work. This was capital W-O-R-K, work. And I'm sure you will agree with me after you hear "The rest of the story."

Generally speaking, most of the homes in Alaska burned #3 diesel fuel both for cooking and heating purposes. A 53 gallon drum of fuel usually carried one household for a period of several weeks or so. Therefore, one might figure that four or five drumsfull should sustain an average household for a period of several months before it became necessary for them to replenish their fuel supply.

Craig, unfortunately for me, rested upon a hill. Not a high one mind you, but nevertheless a hill quite capable of creating a gut puller under the right conditions, and those conditions were soon to show themselves. There was a number of families living on the opposite side of the hill from downtown Craig who were more than anxious to find someone who would deliver oil to their homes, but the question was whom? My name certainly was not whom by choice, but apparently I did fill the bill. Rather than whom, I know now that Cheechako would have been a far more appropriate name at the time.

Good ol' Bailey provided me with a hand truck for free, outa the goodness of his heart. It was a two-wheeled dolly especially designed with a u-shaped frame in order to match the round profile of an oil drum. In addition to that, it was also was equipped with a unique hook attachment. The hook was used to steady an oil drum so that hopefully, it would not roll off the hand truck while it was being transported. **I Was In Business!** All I had to do was go down to the oil dock located downtown, load an oil drum filled with 53 gallons of diesel fuel onto my little old hand truck, then truck it over the hill for whomever had placed an order for such a delivery. Boy was I in luck. Demand for the product is the key to any business, right? Out of the eighteen residences on the other side of the hill, a mere eighteen of them requested my services.

A full drum of oil weighed 400 lbs. So heaven help you if one rolled off the hand truck because it became a near impossibility to load it back on by yourself. Coming off the oil dock, it was nice and flat, was duck soup, but when I started up the hill. Whooooie! It took better than an hour for me to wrestle that first drum of oil (over the hill to grandma's house.) Of course that is discounting my wheezing, gasping and resting time. "I soon discovered that braying helped a lot."

Amazingly I became quite adept at handling these strenuous loads, so eventually, was able to make a delivery in less than forty-five minutes time. I received $5.00 for each drum delivered and it wasn't very long before I was making $25.00 to $30.00 a day. Then at the same time, I was developing a Charles Atlas physique absolutely free with no cost to myself whatsoever outside of an enlarged heart, a nice set of varicose veins, and a powerful pair of lungs which I capitalized on by taking up playing the harmonica.

I was kept quite busy for a matter of several months hauling oil, while in addition to that I received numerous requests to perform other tasks, such as splitting wood, painting, and minor maintenance work. In no time at all I had become a noted handyman around town. Thinking back on the time when I panicked over not seeing any work in sight, all I can say is pshaw! I have so much work lined up ahead of me at this point in time, I think I would prefer to be punching a time clock on an eight hour basis.

What was bewildering to me was the fact that, although I didn't have what one would call a steady job, I never found myself without a nice pocketful of change. Of course this was due to the fact that I had no rent to pay, had no charge accounts to speak of, and electricity was furnished by the city for $22.50 per month.

I would allude to the fact that the fringe benefits associated with my not having a steady job, far outweighed those that I might have received from any job I might have had prior to my arrival in Alaska. Almost everyone I worked for showed their appreciation for my helping them by invariably offering me a cup of coffee followed by, - - "Oh, I just baked a cake. Won't you please take some home with you?" or, "Slim Seltzer just dropped off a big halibut, it's far more than we could possibly use." Then in the same breath would commence carving off a nice big 15 lb. hunk, for me to take home to the Mrs. Honestly, it became an everyday occurrence that some person or another offered me some form of amenities for my work. Bailey oft times sent me home with fresh eggs or a chicken now and then. Others offered clams, crab, deer, etc. Honest to Pete, so many people that willing to share. It became a habit for me to neglect to charge for my work as a gesture to reciprocate for their many kindness'.

Hadn't I mentioned that Bailey was the magistrate for the town of Craig. Hadn't I also mentioned that he had sent me home with a chicken now and then. Apparently I had forgotten to mention that Bailey raised chickens as a supplement to his magistrates salary. Herein lies some pretty good story tellin. Bailey's hen house contained upward of 250 dumb chickens. I was hired by Bailey to clean out the hen house and to then spread fresh hay over the entire floor of the building when I was through. This was to be done on a weekly basis. Well now, on this particular day I had the hen house all cleaned up and was in the act of spreading fresh hay over the floor. Incidentally this was the dumb chickens favorite sport, crowding and pushing to the front so as to grab the loose seeds as they fell from the hay as I spread it around.

Believe me, a couple hundred chickens can sure make a lot of racket when all are scrambling for the seed at the same time. However, it was nothing compared to the hell that broke loose right after I had stuck my pitchfork into a new bale. A huge rat burst out of the bale and headed pell mell for who knows where? Imagine the havoc caused by hundreds of dumb chickens going berserk, while they emitted ear shattering squawking noises, then commenced to jump and beat their wings in a frenzy at the sight of a rat attacking them. I have my doubts that the rat was attacking, he just wanted to get the heck out of there.

While all the other dumb chickens were turning 'chicken,' one old Rhode Island Red hen zeroed in on Mr. Rat. She followed his frantic antics to escape, her head darting from side to side matching his every move until that time when the rat was within striking distance. Suddenly, with a lightning like strike her bill went thump on the floor and Mr. Rat ceased living right then and there.

I was aghast! Considering all the noise and confusion caused by the 'chicken' chickens, combined with the speed of that rat, this was truly an amazing fete for the hen to have accomplished. I had never ever heard of anything like this let alone actually bear witness to such a thing, but all the chickens knew. No sooner had the rat ceased living, the whole flock settled down to resume searching for stray grass seeds just as though nothing had happened. As soon as I was able, I picked up the rat to check it out. Much to my amazement it was obvious that the red hen had unerringly nailed the rat right through the brain in that one split second, that's all there was to it.

Man, oh man, it took quite a little bit of time before I became unnerved enough to hunt down Bailey and confront him with this awesome event. Bailey didn't seem too excited over the incident but did offer me an explanation. "Oh, yeah, I remember that red hen. She's got a brood of chicks right now and she was acting in defense of them young'uns. A Mama hen is a tough cookie when it comes to caring for her babies." I've definitely changed my mind about constantly referring to the chickens as being dumb. I'm actually more inclined to grant that the rat was the dumb one.

TIME AND TIDE

I'm sure you'll be glad you came along for this phase of our, "Journey to Alaska." In this chapter you will learn to understand how important a role the tides play for those people who live by the water. Here we go!

After having gotten settled in Craig but for a short time, Cal came over one evening to visit and to offer me an opportunity to pick up a couple hundred extra bucks if I were interested. Ho! Ho! Do duckies like water?

Because of the high tides that had occurred during the previous week, along with a series of gusty winds, the boathouse belonging to the U.S. Forest service had broken loose from it's moorings and was now stranded high and dry on the beach at the cove. The Forest Service had offered Cal $500.00 if he could somehow find the means to refloat it on the next series of high tides which would occur during the upcoming weekend.

This is when Cal offered me $200.00 of the lump sum if I would help him with this really tough task. Quite naturally I accepted his offer due to the fact that it was a real challenge, although I was fully aware that secondly, along with the challenge, there was $200.00 involved. Cal advised me that he was accepting a like amount for his share, and that the remaining $100.00 would be used in purchasing whatever materials we deemed necessary to complete the job. Fair enough!

Cal and I immediately settled down to have a meeting of the minds, then finally came up with a plan that, although it involved a great deal of hard work, lent us hope that the fruits of our labor would spell success.

Our plan was to scour the town for as many unused oil drums we could muster, making certain they were empty with all the bungs in place and securely tightened. (The bung in an oil drum is the same as a plug in a cask, except that these bungs were threaded, allowing them availability for removal whenever it was necessary to insert a pump in order to expel the oil from the drum.) We intended to lash as many of these oil drums all around and in between the huge spruce logs upon which the boathouse rested. Our reasoning was that since a drum of oil weighed 400 lbs, that same drum in the water, airtight, would do just the opposite and lift 400 lbs.

Our working hours were governed by the action of the tides. We started working each night on an outgoing tide, then kept at it right on through the night until the tide had reached it's low, and had then started back towards it's high the following morning. We worked diligently each night for five nights straight until that time when we had every conceivable surface where we could attach a drum, covered, and even then we hung a few more by lashing them to the ones that were already lashed.

The highest tide for this particular week was to be on Friday. Unfortunately for us it was to be seven tenths of a foot lower than the tide had been that fateful night when the float house had been tossed onto the beach. We were hoping that it would have been a plus seven tenths of a foot rather than a minus seven tenths, because believe you me we needed every ounce of lift we could muster to help float this gargantuous monstrosity off the beach. Cal and I were both cognizant of the fact that if we didn't manage to refloat the, "Thing," on this tide, we were doomed. The next batch of plus tides were a good month away, while at the same time the Forest Service insisted that they needed the boathouse, N-O-W!

Altogether we had managed to salvage and lash to the undercarriage of the float logs, something in the neighborhood of from 35 to 40 oil drums. Granted that each drum would afford 400 lbs. of lift apiece, we felt assured that we could raise 16,000 lbs., eight tons, with just the drums alone. We assumed that the big spruce logs on which the main structure was sitting would most assuredly do their part towards floating the boathouse off the beach when it came time to pull her free from the mud flat. Because of the fact that the spruce logs under the structure had been drying on the beach for a period of time, we felt confident that they would float much higher than when they were first beached.

Spruce logs have a tendency to float many times higher in the water than any other type of wood, especially when they're dry. This was truly, for us, a blessing in disguise because we sure needed every speck of help we could get in our final effort towards gaining even a crumb more of help. We then focused our attention on the end of the boathouse that was facing the incoming tide. We accomplished this by stacking additional drums one on top of another, then lashing them securely to the existing drums, thus once more gaining a small but critical bit more lift of 4,000 lbs.

Two more nights to go till high tide. We were thinking how simple it would have been had we been doing this job stateside, rather than here. All of this labor and agony would have been unnecessary. All we would have had to do was call in a tug, and presto! Tug! Holy smokes, now there's a poignant idea. Libby, McNeil, and Libby has a salmon cannery here in Craig, sitting idle waiting for the fishing season to get started in the spring. Also sitting idle in their warehouse was a crab, a B-B winch. Carl Paschen, their caretaker, agreed that we could use the winch, so Cal and I loaded it on a hand truck and trucked it for a quarter mile or so down onto the city float, where we would have access to some pilings for a tailhold. By rigging the B-B winch tight to the float we were able to string the cable to a tow bit, located on the leading end of the boathouse, only a few hundred feet away. Oh happy day!

All is in readiness at long last. It is now approaching three AM on this Friday morning. The tide is creeping forth so softly it is impossible to detect if the water is actually rising, although the whole boathouse structure seems to be afloat in the darkness. There isn't any daylight to speak of and our flashlights are incapable of reaching as far out as the boathouse so that we can see what's going on. According to my tide book, the water shall reach its maximum height at three AM, but it is now 3:10 AM. Could it be possible that we have failed in our efforts? At this time, a wee bit of daylight is commencing to filter in through the darkness of the night. We have put a very intense strain on the winch but can detect no motion from the stubborn behemoth. It is such a disheartening moment for Cal and me. We came so close to success, only to have failure rise up to be our only reward for all that time and effort.

Suddenly a small breeze sprang up. The water that had been glassy smooth developed a bit of chop. The boathouse showed minute signs of movement. We dared to apply just one more ounce of pull on the overtaxed winch, when unbelievably; the whole she-bang came free of the beach. Were we ever elated over this turn of events. Thank God for that timely little breeze or we would never have made it. All that was left for us to do was horse it into the float, make it secure, then sit down completely flabbergasted that we had beaten the odds.

How about it folks. Aren't you glad you got in on that one?

NO SEE UM

Hi folks. I just received some interesting statistics from one of the local natives as we were standing on the float after our launching of the ark. Ya wanna hear it? Sorry, the ayes have the vote! So here it comes anyway.

The friendly native asked me if I was aware of the fact that the origination of the name, Alaska, came from the Russian version of the word Aleutian, pronounced (Alakshak} by the Russians, which meant Peninsula, Great Land, or Land That Is Not An Island.

Another tidbit he wished to offer and well worth mentioning, was Alaska embraces six distinct Indian nations, which include the Eskimo, the Aleut, the Athabascan, the Haida, the Thlinget, and finally the Tsimpsians. He also volunteered that there was a lot of speculation still going on concerning the status of the Eskimo as to whether they should be called Indians or Mongols. Some part of their history defines them as migrants from Mongolia who crossed the Northernmost Ice Caps eons ago, then settled in what was know as Alakshak at that point in time. Personally I'm uncertain as to whether Russia actually owned Alaska during the ice age period. To me, that seems too early to be the case. Maybe some one of you can do some research on this and come up with an answer, okay?

I think we're in luck. Our Indian statistician is offering to tell us a real Indian Legend, because as we're standing on the float everyone seems to be itching and scratching, although there are no signs of mosquitoes or other flying creatures around. I shall endeavor to duplicate the manner in which he speaks. It is perfectly understandable, but kinda different in the way it is presented because he does butcher the Kings English to a certain extent.

This is how he starts his story. (Quote:) "It was a long, long time, when my grandfather told me of this very evil spirit comed to his village to live with them and hunt with them. No one know he is an evil spirit cause he come to us and tell us he belong to the other Thinget village that everyone got sick and died, so he is alone and wants to become one of us."

"First, because he is evil, he make the wind blow extra hard and it knock down many tents where the fish and deer meat is hung for to be dried before the winter come. One time he makes the rain come down hard at the same time we having the big pow-wow, so it puts out the fire what is cooking the pot-luck dinner for everybody. Now because he is evil, nobody can enjoy the celebration with the banquet. Everyone is wondering that the Gods must be upset with them from something, they don't know for sure what it tis. One time one of the people seened the stranger beating on the water with a big stick upstream from where the tribe is fishing for the fish to dry and smoke, but the evil one has scared all the fish away. When they tell the Chief, he is suspicious by now about the new one, so he's going to the medicine man. The medicine man tells him yes, he has heard of such an evil one like this one, who always does evil things like all them ones what the Chief has heard about from his people. The medicine man promised that he would speak with the Gods to find out what to do. The next day our Shaman told it to the Chief. The Gods telled me he will get worse, he might kill some of us unless we can destroy this evil thing before he gets more powerful. Right away, the next day they captured the evil one and hunged him by the neck, but the rope broke, so he got away. Now he's got mad. Some of the men tricked him to go in the boat to go fishing. Then they got him all tangled up with the anchor lines and made an accident like the boat tipped over. Everyone got dumped in the water but the ropes comed off the evil one so he didn't got drowned."

Thus far into the story our friendly Thlinget native has captured our complete attention so we continue to suffer through the nuisancesome insect attacks while he resumes telling his story.

"Now everyone knows he has got madder and more powerful just like the Shaman said he would. "Don't try to trick him anymore," he warned them. "You must take your bows and arrows and your spears to kill him, right now. The tribe's best hunters waited by the trail. Then when he comed by they shot him with their arrows and stabbed him with their spears, but he put a strong spell on their weapons so all the arrows bounced off and the spears broke in half, making the evil one to laugh at them. Now he began to do worse things to them. Many tents blew away. Some children died when they were born, making the women sad, really bad things like that. "

It was becoming somewhat uncomfortable standing here on the float, scratching away while constantly being bitten by an unseen gnat or whatever, but we were enthralled with the story, so we all hung in there listening intently as he went on.

"The medicine man prayed to the Gods one more time to help his people. "You must shoot the evil one in the foot, with the arrow," they told him, "Because he made himself stronger some more, that is the only place where he is not safe on his body." "This they did and he fell to the ground, dead!" "This is not enough," he warned them, "You must get rid of him, all. You will build a big, big fire to throw him in and you won't be bothered with him some more." "After they did all this and the fire was all burned up they searched for any signs of him, but there was nothing. Even the bones was gone, too."

"That night the strong wind came in so nobody noticed it, and lifted the ashes way up to the sky, then they all coming back down like teeny little specks that you can't see. This one we call No-See-Um. When they land on you, you gonna itch and scratch so hard, sometimes you gonna bleed. Now they have founded out they didn't destroy the evil spirit all the way. His ashes are keep coming back, what are no-see-ums, and they are still doing evil things to you."

Then, while harboring a big old grin on his face, he handed us the finale! "If you don't want to believe what I tell you, then right now, how come you feelum the no-see-um, but still you no-see-um?"

SCAT CAT

Okay gang, we're going big cat hunting today, but not quite like we would had I talked you into an African journey.

It was less than two weeks time following the rat in the hen house incident, when Bailey sent word he needed to see me. Because of Bailey's influence, I had joined the Moose Club during the interim, so assumed that Bailey perhaps wanted to discuss some part of my application with me.

What's this! He wants me to kill a cat?

It seemed that an old maverick tomcat had started molesting his chickens, mostly for sport as Bailey put it, because they were simply slaughtered, then left uneaten. He appeared to be really upset, since the attacks on the chicks were developing into becoming a daily habit for the cat. "John boy," he pleaded. "I want ya to get that damned animal for me, my eye sight ain't like it used to be. I see that lousy tom most every morning right around ten O'clock. He sneaks out from behind that brush yonder, then kinda slinks along that low spot to the right there where I can't get a good look at him. I figure you might get him for me on account'a you got good eyes."

The following morning I showed up a little early so we could plan our strategy. While Bailey's wife Francis brewed us a pot of coffee, we set up an observation post where we could keep our eyes peeled for the chicken killer.

Sure enough, Sandy had it figured right. Sandy is the name Bailey prefers to use when he's asking a favor of someone. Claims it's a lot more personal than Bailey. It's also short for his last name, Sandifer.

Hmmff? Anyway, Sandy had it pegged right as to the time and place for the big hunt. It was two minutes until 10 AM. when we spotted the big yellow tomcat creeping toward the hen house just as Sandy had predicted it would.

We were ready for him. Sandy and I watched tensely as the villainous predator slunk low to the ground with it's ears laid back and it's eyes focused straight ahead towards it's objective, cautiously inching forward just as a lioness would do in stalking her prey.

I elbowed Sandy then whispered, "I got it figured out he's gonna come out right about there," as I pointed to a large clump of wild rhubarb. I cradled the 32 Winchester rifle Sandy had provided me tight in my arms, trained my sights just at the very edge of the rhubarb patch, then right at the moment the killer cat's head showed, moved my sights about an inch ahead, then touched off the shot.

(Music and chimes, here) One leap straight up, then plop, down he come, ne'er to run again, when the old tom died. At the same time Sandy bellered, "Diggety, dog, yah got him, yah got him," jarring me loose from my beautiful Grandfather's Clock song. I'll bet you can't possibly imagine what happened right after that shot was fired.

GRATITUDITY PLUS

In the previous chapter I remember mentioning that we joined the Moose Lodge, here in Craig. In this chapter we shall become familiarized with the close knit fellowship all Moose members extend towards one another. Their continually aspiring to project brotherly love and truthfulness, besides compassion, and honesty towards their lodge brothers.

So now let us continue from the previous chapter.

Nailing that lousy tom for Sandy wasn't the only thing I nailed, judging from the racket coming out of the hen house right after I fired at that darn cat. At first we thought the noise from the gun being fired had scared the daylights out of the chickens, causing them to go bonkers again. Rather than that when we went inside the hen house to investigate, something unimaginable had taken place. When I had nailed that damned tom for Sandy, the bullet from my shot had gone clean on through the cat, penetrating the hen house but also clipping one leg apiece off of three different chickens.

Now there's one for you! Imagine if you will the turmoil being created by the three one-legged chickens squawking and beating their wings in a frenzy, while going round and round in circles but actually getting nowhere in spite of all their effort. (Sandy demanded that we call him Bailey at this particular time, for what reason, I have no idea) Therefore, Bailey found it necessary to compound the commotion even on a higher plain as he strived to capture the one-legged hens. Amidst a cloud of feathers, a whole tribe of excited chickens and a few expletives from Bailey, the capture was eventually brought to a conclusion when miraculously, in a matter of minutes, the hen house had settled down from calamity to calm, once again.

Surprisingly, Bailey seemed to keep his cool over the incident with his only comment being, "Well, it would be a real shame to waste all that meat, so John boy, why don't you and the Mrs. come on over for dinner tomorrow night?" "My wife Franny will put on the most fantastic chicken and dumplings feed you'll ever wrap your gums around." "What do you say to that?" Hells Fire, man! My mamma didn't raise any dummies. Of course I accepted. Wasn't I obligated as a friend, to help him not waste all that meat?

Believe me, it did turn out to be an exceptionally fine dinner since, as I felt compelled to mention, there certainly was an abundance of real yummy chicken in the pot.

All during the meal there was a good deal of bantering and joking over the fantastic shot I had made, how everything had all turned out so well, besides having ended up with such a scrumptious meal and a bundle of laughs thrown in to boot.

Oh sure, gullible John boy. I was to discover at a later date that all this laughter and good-natured comrade was in reality, oh so hideously false.

Would you believe this kindly and generous old man took me to court in spite of the good turn I had so generously and spontaneously performed for him, in order to save his chicks.

For my own protection, I wish for you to bear witness that I had joined the Moose long before this fowl tasting dinner, thereby establishing myself as a brother, because! During the Lodge Meeting nights, there is one special session entitled, "For The Good Of The Order!" This is when Bailey put the sting on me as he stepped forward to confront his fellow Moose Brothers with a tale of woe while he presented his case against me. He immediately commenced with the alligator tears bit, while at the same time elaborating on the injustice I had heaped upon his poor old bony shoulders. "Brothers," he pleaded, "Imagine if you will, a fellow brother going so far as to disable three of my finest laying hens in order to guarantee that he would be rewarded for doing nothing more than an act of brotherly love from one brother to another. He then reiterated the history of the tom, the chickens, and the exquisite dinner, which followed. Oh,oh, me thinks I detected a number of oohs and ahs coming from the court of my peers following this declaration.

In addition to all this, Bailey laid claim that I had caused him personal anguish and grief since he was forced to destroy those three fine hens that he loved very dearly. "Wait a minute," I tried to counter, "What d'ya mean, loved a chicken?" but I was shushed and told my rebuttle would come later.

Bailey maintained that since he kept a clean and comfortable hen house for his chickens, right there was evidence enough that he was very fond of them, right? "People love dogs and cats." "Do dogs and cats contribute to anyone's source of income?" "Hell no." "Do chickens? "Ya damn right, so why shouldn't I love'em?

He presented his case with unabashed passion, the danged old flap mouth. I call him this because for further affect he even went so far as to remove his falsies so that he stood bowed and broken, the perfect picture of a sad and demoralized cotton pickin chicken farmer. He shoulda got a movie contract out of it, wow what a performance.

I might have been a little naïve but somehow I'm beginning to think, something smells fowl around here because the court made up entirely of Moose members concluded that I had done Bailey a grave injustice. I pleaded on bended knee that there was no way in Hell I could possibly have known in advance that my kindly act toward my Moose brother would in any way, shape or form, lead to causing him grief or anguish. Now in addition to all this my brothers of the Moose, my very good friends, my lodge companions, "Knock It Off," came a voice from the rear. "Flattery will get you nowheres, brother." Nevertheless, I continued on in my own defense. "After all, didn't I save Bailey a heap of dough in the event that he felt compelled to buy me a nice dinner for all I had done for him. What do you suppose a dinner like that would have cost him in town?

Oh well! my sentence didn't turn out to be too harsh after all. I was ordered to split a sufficient supply of wood for Gramma Gunyah that would last her throughout the upcoming winter, since it was already starting into November. Hah! Did I ever have the last laugh on them? Unbeknownst to the court I had already consigned myself to that little chore.

The last laugh as it turned out, didn't prove to be the last laugh after all.

Their timing was perfect. The Moose Lodge annual Thanksgiving day banquet, was the upcoming event on the calendar for this month. This was a real spiffy event, where the guys put on real shirts and wore ties, rather than boots and mackinaws as they were accustomed to wearing. So here we are, it's Thanksgiving evening at last. Wow, what a beautiful setup the Ladies of the Moose have prepared. Pretty candles lent a warm glow on the serving table but in addition to that, would you believe there were several bouquets of very rare, real live flowers from Heaven only knows where. The ladies, all of them sporting dresses and with their hair all done up nice, looked exceptionally pretty since we were accustomed to seeing them in jeans most of the time. The dinner service proved to be equally as lavish as the rest of the festivities. Each guest was being served individually by the ladies, who dished up heaping helpings of creamy mashed potatoes and gravy, along with mouth watering wild cranberries, sweet potatoes, and big juicy slabs of turkey with dressing. Get the picture.

Somehow my serving didn't show up until the very last, but certainly not least. I was presented with a platter heaped high with an old leather boot, all shrinkley looking, steaming hot, and in addition to that, what an aroma. I can honestly say, the odor was far from conducive to whetting one's appetite. At this point the story about the chicken incident was passed about and elaborated on in order to clarify for all those present that I had indeed already eaten a superb dinner consisting of Frances Sandifer's delectable chicken and dumplings. Therefore, I was not entitled to another nice dinner quite this soon.

See, Didn't I tell you that in this chapter we would learn from the Moose their eagerness to exemplify, compassion, honesty, and all those qualities necessary for becoming leaders in the community?

Thank goodness, because of this rare quality, I was eventually served a much nicer smelling portion of Thanksgiving fare.

A WHALE BALLET

Today I shall share with you a whale of a good time, which I'm sure will add to the unusual series of events that you have so far experienced in this, your journey to "An Alaska you never imagined, existed."

Wally Johnson, a Thlinget Indian friend of mine, has us venturing forth this morning in search of the mighty king, the biggest and sportiest of all the several varieties of salmon found in these Alaskan waters.

It would be amazing to me if any of you might recall the old outmoded, nine and three quarter horse, long shanked Johnson outboard motor. Would you believe it; that is exactly what we are using to propel our rather small, fourteen foot skiff, scurrying along at a speed in excess of three knots. A short shanked outboard was introduced at a later date in order to compensate for the fact that the long-shanked motor hit bottom too soon when beaching. Hitting bottom was a no-no because it snapped the shear pin, which as expressed in nautical terms, left you dead in the water. The shear pin was actually engineered to do just that! "Snap!" so that you would not ruin the propeller in the event that you did hit bottom. It was always possible, although it was a nuisancesome task to install another shear pin. However, in the event that you sheared a blade off the prop, you were just plain out and out stranded.

Running through six miles of open water in a fourteen-foot skiff, boy did I think that was something. To the Thlinget Indians this was simply a way of life. We managed to encounter quite a variety of sea-life as we roared slowly along, and that included both land otters and sea otters. We also saw seals, sea lions, and hundreds of sea birds on our way to an island, bearing the Spanish name San Juan Batista, which means St John The Baptist, and this would ultimately be our final destination to start fishing for King Salmon. Adjoining the big island was a much smaller one called little St John. In fact there are a number of areas in and around South Eastern Alaska bearing Spanish names because at some point in time the Spaniards invaded Alaska with the idea of adopting the land themselves.

We had rounded San Juan Batista on the North side and were preparing to begin trolling for King Salmon. Suddenly and without any indication of it's presence a submarine surfaced right beside our skiff emitting a terrifying kind of woosh sound, scaring us half out of our socks. Immediately thereafter, we detected a huge eye glaring at us not more than fifty feet away. "Holy smokeries, that's a whale," I gasped. I swear it looked as big as a submarine, it was that close to us.

The whale gave us the once over as he affixed that one huge eye on our little teeny skiff, then slipped quietly beneath the water and was gone. Wally sprang into action, immediately gunning the throttle on our speedy three knots per hour craft, then headed for shore at once. He obviously was concerned for our safety. The channel was narrow but very deep so it took us no time at all to reach shore, when after dragging our skiff out of the water where we could be safe on land, we centered our attention back to where we had seen the whale surface.

What a sight! They surely took us by surprise, when two whales burst up out of the water, literally standing on their tails belly to belly and in the same spot we had seen the first one. They splashed back down into the water with such force as to create huge waves that most assuredly would have swamped our skiff, had we not gotten the Hell out'a there when we did. Wally expostulated excitedly as he jumped up and down genuinely happy to be alive. "See, I knowed we are in trouble," he shouted. "This is the mating dance for the whales. Sometimes that male whale is going to show off to the lady whale so if we are there he might take his tail to flip us way up in the air. He can do the whole boat and us too just to show the lady whale how strong he is. We are very lucky the shore was close to us or he might have done this thing." We weren't sure if the whales were able to copulate in this manner because it was for only a brief interval that they had contact with one another.

Nonetheless, we were quite disappointed that the whales failed to reappear following that one unbelievable display.

However, we shall always carry it in our minds as one of those rare experiences when we were where we weren't supposed to be at the right time.

So my fellow travelers there you have it, another singularly and rare encounter, definitely not offered through any travel folders that I know of.

A DAMSEL IN DISTRESS

We've gotten ourselves into a fine mess this time and I'm afraid it's going to take a lot of work if we're to dig ourselves out.

Her name is Mayreld Swanson, the wife of the Presbyterian minister here in Craig. You've got to keep in mind that was she one of those who welcomed us to stay right after we arrived in Craig for the first time. She was one of those who had offered sheets and bedding, etc. otherwise we might be inclined to turn up our noses and refuse to help her in this, her hour of need. Therefore, I guess we're obligated and that's final.

It all started innocently enough when Mayreld called me one evening to inform me she was having sewer problems, would I please come over in the morning and check it out. Oh, oh, I'm already inclined to check out but in Alaska, "We help each other." Thanks Billy Chuck, for reminding me of that one.

The following morning I showed up for a preliminary inspection only to discover the whole system to be plugged up. Even the pipes leading to the septic tank were rusted through to the extent that the affluents from the bathroom weren't even entering the tank at all, but rather than that were backing up to the sewer. To make matters worse, the tank itself was actually rusting away as well.

Upon informing Mayreld as to what I had uncovered, she turned red in the face while shamefully admitting she had been suspicious that this would prove to be the case. Then she brightened up and almost in the same breath volunteered that she had already ordered a new tank to replace the old one and that it would be on the next boat to arrive from Seattle, the following week. Now wasn't that good news? Yeah, but for whom?

Actually there was no one in town capable of helping her since all the able bodied guys were out fishing, leaving nothing more than grocery clerks and bar tenders available for anything as hairy as this, so!

This is just a teeny remote little town, harboring no such things as ditch diggers and mechanized equipment sitting around readily available for a job of this magnitude, so there's no doubt in my mind: "This is definitely going to be a pick and shovel show." Wow! I'm already visualizing the amount of excessive hand digging this little project is gonna require. I know for certain that it will be necessary to enlarge the area surrounding the tank to a point where a man would be able to stand beside the tank in order to swing a pick and use a shovel in his excavating process? (Think, man, think!) I've simply got to come up with something that doesn't demand all that shovel work, but what?

First off, I went to work exposing the whole of the top of the tank and maybe not quite half of each side. This afforded me access to all the fittings, which I then methodically proceeded to plug air-tight. I had previously thumped on the tank and determined that it was leaking on the bottom to some extent, therefore it couldn't have been too full. My next trick was to run a garden hose down under the tank as far as it would go, then turned the water on and let it run for a couple of days when sure enough, the tank suddenly popped up out of the hole looking like a radically designed ghost ship sitting on an invisible ocean. Boy, did it ever look big in comparison to how small it appeared to be when buried in the ground. Following this stroke of luck, I immediately hooked onto the tank from the downhill side and yanked it outa there with a B-B winch. Yep, you guessed it. The same good old B-B winch I had described in a previous chapter, when Cal and I did the boat house job.

Let's hold it for a minute, right here. Sure, the tanks out of the hole, but we're not done with this li'l project by a damsite. How about all the water that is left in the hole where the tank sat? It figures, if I flooded the hole with water by means of a hose, shouldn't I simply reverse the process? That's it! I strung out several lengths of hose on the downhill side of our mini-lake and used them as a syphon in place of a pump. Hot diggety dog, it worked. In just two days, by employing this method, we managed to drain the hole sufficiently enough for me to go ahead with enlarging it to the point where it could now accommodate the new tank.

Remember, I told you at the beginning of the chapter we'd have to work hard to dig our way out of this one? So what else, ya gotta start digging brother. Good, I've finally managed to enlarge the hole to something like five feet square and seven foot deep. It sure wasn't easy. Maybe you all can guess why. It so happened I was forced to shovel dirt that was impregnated with, this dirt was impregnated with, let's say, "Man alive did it ever give off a lot of gas." And for that reason I was compelled to pop up out of the hole quite frequently when I ran out of gas, mainly because of the excess amount of gas where I was working. At this point in time I was thoroughly convinced, "There is nothing in this world offering a sweeter fragrance than that wonderful Alaska air I was afforded, each and every time I popped up out of that stinkin hole in the ground. Amen, brother.

To make a long story short, the tank arrived from Seattle as scheduled, and the installation proved to be successful. However, by today's standards and in looking back on this one, I have my doubts if this job was really worth the $250.00 I was awarded after the new tank was installed and operable. Let's say, just as the Alaska Fairy waved her magic Wand over me, so did she wave it over Mayreld Swanson, and let it go at that.

QUEENIE

 The fandango of events being presented in this chapter are mainly about, "We all help each other", and scrambling for scrambled eggs.
 Today is a beautiful day in our little town of Craig. It seems that everyone is busily engaged in catching up on those things that old man winter had forced them to put aside.
 As I said, today was a beautiful day for most of the residents of Craig but definitely not for me. I'd just gotten a slab of wood in the form of a gargantuous sliver, imbedded in the palm of my hand.
 This happened at the time when Army Armstrong, the district forest ranger who was stationed here at the Cove, hired me to replace some decking on the porch of the Forest Service building. We were in the process of unloading the decking from a truck when one piece of decking started to fall as it was being shoved down to me. As I grabbed for it, wouldn't you know, it just happened to be one of those ugly ones with a splintered edge so one big old sliver lancinated itself into my hand on the fly, then broke off, deeply imbedded in the palm of my hand. It was really a good-sized hunk, much too large to ignore, so we were forced to take action and try to do something about it.
 Since we had no doctors in town most emergency situations were handled by the Coast Guard, which meant that the normal procedure was for the Coast Guard to send in a large rescue plane to haul you into Ketchikan for treatment. However, we did have a retired dentist residing here in Craig but when we confronted him with the injury he felt he wasn't capable of extracting a slab as large as this one, especially since it

was imbedded too darn deep. Even though the dentist was fearful of trying to remove the sliver, the consensus of opinion was steadfast. It wouldn't be quite right to call in the Coast Guard since the emergency wasn't of such drastic proportions as to warrant sending in a large amphibious plane because of a sliver. "OH YEAH! Who in Hell do you think has the sliver, anyway?" That was my immediate thought. I'm telling you straight. This thing was starting to hurt more and more and was beginning to get me spooked a little. After all, one isn't granted a record-breaking sliver like this one very often during a lifetime.

As a last resort someone of my sympathetic bystanders thought of Queenie and suggested that I go see her. She would probably have the courage to dig it out.

Queenie turned out to be a local fisherman's wife who lived aboard a small double-ended troller no more than 22 ft. in length. It was permanently secured to the float at the cove since they seldom went trolling any longer because of their ages, and also because her husband was not well.

I proceeded as I was directed, eventually ending up at the float, found the boat, and found Queenie. I introduced myself, stated my case, and was invited aboard. Her husband Jack Viant, was away at the time, otherwise I am certain there would not have been room for me. Talk about cramped quarters but this is Alaska and you know better than to wonder why.

Queenie was skinny, old, and scrawny looking, but she exemplified that wonderful example of Northern Hospitality as she commanded. "Set yourself down there and have a cup of coffee while I have a look at that hand." After snatching an empty cup from the cluttered table, she leaned down to disengage a well used wool sock from a dilapidated pair of old rubber boots.

Queenie looked me smack dab straight in the eye as she proceeded to wipe out the cup with the old dirty sock, and I knew right there and then that I was being challenged to the fabric of my being by one of the old established sourdoughs of the North. Was I still a Cheechako in her eyes, or had I conformed to the way of the land? I didn't blink an eyelid as she drew a nice steaming hot cup of coffee and handed it to me. Secretly though, I was thinking, "Thank God it's steaming hot. Perhaps that fact alone will save my life." I did myself proud by having enough good sense to say thank you. After having seemingly passed the test, Queenie commenced prattling on about she was already aware that we were new in town and she was sure very anxious to meet my wife.

She also informed me that in the spring, Libby commenced to do pre-season work at their cannery, which at this particular time was sitting idle at one end of town. In addition to that, she, as well as Bailey, both liked the cut of my jib, therefore since they knew Libby's Superintendent quite well, they were going to put in a good word for me to get hired when the work started. "How about that?" At this particular moment in time one John Thompson made the transition from Cheechako to Sourdough. Thank you sliver, (I think!)

Even though I have exceptionally great bladder control mind you, all during the time Queenie was chattering away she had hold of my sliver hand-squeezing and probing about, and this caused me to, in spite of myself, tinkle a little, but I did manage to keep it to myself.

"Well John, I guess we can get the bugger out without your having to fly into Ketchikan," was her final diagnosis. "Just the same, I want you to drink this first," she insisted, as she poured me a whole dang glassful of booze and said, "Down it." She continued to stall and to visit until that time when I was kinda oozing outa my chair then commenced to carve and dig with an old pocketknife that had been laying on the table close by. Incidentally, she wiped the knife-blade clean on the leg of her wool trousers, to make it sanitary don't you reckon? The carving bit did hurt some, but I guess I was numb enough, since I can only vaguely remember when she assisted me in slithering off the boat, so's I wouldn't bounce off the float, as she put it.

I dunno, somehow and sometime later I found myself at home at last. The wound wasn't too sore for a couple of days simply because I had such a damn headache and was hung over so bad from the (sedative?) that I felt no pain elsewhere in my body but my head. It's a wonder to me that everything healed well, there was no sign of an infection, and I ended up with a scar that barely shows at all.

The following incident is not related to this particular period in time. Nevertheless, since it concerns my association with Queenie I will present the story to you as part of an Alaska you never dreamed existed.

It was a long time after the sliver extraction that I did find work at the cannery, and as Queenie had predicted, I did see her in the mess hall nearly every day where she worked as a waitress. It has been many years since this little fiasco occurred so I feel it is appropriate to bring it up now because there is no possibility it can do any harm at this late date.

It had to do with one morning when I was asked to deliver a spatula to the mess house cook after some one of the cannery machinists had riveted a new handle onto it. It was rapidly nearing breakfast time for the cannery crew and Cookie was more than anxious to get hold of the spatula in order to dish up his platters of scrambled eggs. All was post-haste as I rushed in with the tool and believe me, Cookie wasted not one second in loading the platters in time for breakfast.

I had already turned and started out the door, when I heard a loud clatter behind me. I spun around to see what happened, and there was Queenie on her hands and knees, frantically scooping a heap of scrambled eggs from the messy, mess house floor, back onto the platter that had slipped from her grasp. She swiftly plopped them onto the table just as the triangle was jangling for the guys to come and get it. Come and get it they did, stampeding in for chow like a horde of starving loggers. I actually had to get out of the way quick, or get knocked over.

It was simply too late to do anything about the situation, as those eggs, went the way of all good eggs in nothing flat and with no one being the wiser.

I've actually kept my mouth shut for a long, long time because I felt that I owed Queenie one.

Queenie! I've oft times wondered where she got that name?

Betcha it would make one Helluva story!

ALASKA THE BEAUTIFUL

If you've ever visualized Alaska as a cold, covered with ice, windy, chilly place to be, just wait until you see the real beauty of this wondrous land become exposed here in Southeast Alaska shortly after spring pops in. The residents of the area are not the ones who claim Alaska to be enchanting. It is those who view it 's awesome beauty for the first time that it makes such an impression on.

The transformation from winter into spring is mind boggling because it happens so quickly. It takes place just like a snap of the fingers, almost as though Ma Nature simply throws a switch.

While we were talking about it, Ma nature has thrown the switch. It is spring and along with spring, comes the King. Today, we're going to catch one and you'll be hooked for life. I told you from the very start it would be well worth your while to make this trip North, but with this hunk of adventure thrown in! (the guy with the big belly) "Awright, enough, let's just get going, okay?" Hey, take it easy, fella, I'm only trying to make it as exciting for you as I can.

All right, so its spring. After having spent a busy winter in Craig, we've decided to venture forth to try our luck in landing a nice, big, juicy King Salmon. We chose to go trolling in the channel adjoining Craig on its West side, since it was but a short distance from where I lived. We are being favored this morning with an exceptionally calm and clear day. What a sight! From our position on the water we were exposed to a panoramic combination of both, water and land, which constituted a myriad of islands dotting the waters surface. It was breathtakingly beautiful to say the least. It mattered not which direction we were facing there before our eyes lay some of the most magnificent scenery imaginable, totally incontestable in comparison to anything we had ever seen.

I wish I could I put into words, those words that paint a more grandiose picture in your minds than I'm capable of painting. Here we are, all bunched up in a small skiff completely surrounded by a vastness of water and islands very seldom touched by man. There spread before us were the greenest of green islands scattered about on absolutely motionless waterways, in fact so calm and serene it left us with the illusion it was all a mirage. The islands appeared to be suspended ever so gently on the surface of the water, rather than in it. This actually made the whole picture doubly impressive because we were actually seeing a double mirage due to the mirror–like reflections of everything on or near the water.

Guess I'll just have to be me and say, "Man oh man, this is one helluva lot pertier than a stinkn ol' asphalt highway and let it go at that.

Now, in facing down the channel toward the West, we were able to make out the outline of an island named SanJuan Batista. It appeared somewhat ghost-like sitting in the distance, majestically silhouetted against a radiantly pink sky. Alongside of SanJuan Batista sits little St John it's companion Island, hardly a pimple in comparison to the massiveness of big St John, more commonly called this by those in the area who use these two companion Islands as a guide and landmark.

Incidentally, the channels surrounding the Batista Islands, also harbored the mighty King Salmon. Betcha can't guess where we're headed?

The name King is synonymous with granting these pugilistic salmon their rightful position in the fishing world. Should you hook onto one of these babies you will get the thrill of your life. At the same time, there would be no logical reason for you to wonder why a fisherman who has ever caught one of these ferociously powerful fish, would grant them any other name, but King.

SanJuan Batista dead ahead, pull her hard aport. (steer the skiff left) We've arrived and we're all decked out with a very sturdy ten-foot salmon fishing rod. In addition to that we're sporting an extra large Penn reel loaded to the hilt with 27lb test, monofilament nylon line. On top of all this we're equipped with a special 40lb test stainless steel leader. We felt it necessary to attach this to the end of the line because we had been informed that the King when hooked, will inevitably extend its razor sharp cheek plates and thus sever the line. This little trick of his, falsely leads the angler to believe the monster was so big he broke the line when in reality it had actually cut itself free. Nevertheless, we must be feeling a little bit sheepish, like maybe we weren't showing true sportsmanship in using such overly heavy gear, when suddenly the rod is nearly torn from your grasp as though you had snagged a speed boat. Ya didn't even have to set the hook the strike was so intense and you're now witnessing your line playing off the reel at an alarming rate. You've commenced cranking like mad in order to retrieve your gear, which at this point is better than 50% gone. Immediately following that savage attack, whatever you have on has turned and is coming back towards you at break-neck speed, forcing you to crank even more furiously in order that you allow it no slack. Zzzzzzz, out goes your line again but this time in the opposite direction. In a heartbeat, you manage to tighten the drag a little bit between these high speed relays in order to tire the, what you must realize by now, is a King Salmon. After three or more intense passes there comes a time when unbelievably, you find yourself actually gaining on the defiant fighter at the end of your line.

At this point you've somehow managed to drag your catch up to the side of the boat where it's obvious to see you have caught yourself one big, big looking fish. It took one hell of a lot of tugging and grunting on your part to get this monster aboard without losing it but now the damned fish is really squiggling, wiggling and thrashing about, still determinedly testing his strength against yours.

You are ecstatic, cause lying there at your feet is a beautiful, huge King Salmon, with it's sides glimmering brightly in the sunlight like newly minted coins, but at the same time it's scales are glowing brilliantly purple. The salmon continued thrashing from side to side, defiantly making an effort to knock the bottom out of the skiff. Only after delivering a mighty clout at the base of its head with the gaff hook, are you able to subdue "The King."

What a sight he presented as you gazed upon your prize, quivering with excitement and very near upchucking because of it. It has to be that your heart had lodged against your puker button making you swallow hard to get it back into place. There you have it. The thrill you'll experience the first time you hook onto a King. Incidentally, these babies weigh anywhere from 28 to 100 lbs normally, although Ellis Air in Ketchikan has one mounted on the wall of their terminal that weighed 126 lbs. What a terrific difference compared to the 8-10 oz crappies we are accustomed to catching, stateside.

While we're talking King Salmon, I have an interesting anecdote to pass on to you for your future use should you become an avid King Salmon enthusiast.

It is a common sight when fishing for Kings to witness the salmon actually leap clear out of the water. Its been said that the fish do this in order to rid themselves of the sea lice clinging to their bodies prior to entering a fresh water inlet before the spawning process is undertaken. This is in part, true. However, our

Indian friends do not agree with this theory, entirely. They insist that when they see a jump, the salmon are in the act of feeding. Their expertise has taught them that when the salmon locate a school of needlefish, their favorite food, they circle round and round shaping the school into a ball. After this is accomplished the salmon turns and with a terrific rush shoots up through the ball of needle fish, or herring, one other of their favorite foods, immediately returning to feed upon those that appear to be either stunned or injured. He will repeat these antics until that time when he is sufficiently fed so for this reason the Indian is always on the alert to espy a jump, knowing for sure that this is where he is most likely to encounter, "THE KING!"

I had applied this same theory in catching a King by employing a green and silver elongated plug, much resembling a needlefish both in size and color. However, I had been advised that the King will strike on anything small and shiny, thus any variety of lures may prove to be equally effective, such as a Canadian Wonder, any small silver spoon, or a small herring.

No matter what the lure, if you are successful in landing a King Salmon, there is no doubt in my mind that you will end up feeling like a King, yourself.

DAMMIT

I hope all of you get a kick out of this one, friends!

You know, in looking back on my relationship with Bailey Sandifer, I instinctively search for terms of endearment suitable enough to fit his noble character. So far, all I've been able to come up with is, damn chicken farmer, natural born troublemaker, and City Magistrate. After all, you've got to give him some credit. He did consider it his civil duty when he sent Jimmie Snook who was 55, to the hoosegow for incest of his 80 year old grandmother. The old coot even went so far as to marry his former wife's daughter. Bailey was approaching 70–75 years of age, who knows for sure, when he wed this pretty young thing, at least 30 years younger than he.

It is interesting to note that Totem Poles tell of victories, coupes, and accomplishments attributed to Indian Braves during their lifetimes. Can you imagine the Totem Pole they might construct for this character should the whites elect to adopt Totem Poles as part of their culture.

In the spring, after I began working at the cannery here in Craig, ol' Sandy, that's what everyone called Bailey whenever he wasn't up to some form of deviltry, had it figured out he was about to lose his oil barrel hauling buddy. For this reason he somehow managed to get hold, of all things, a donkey from somewhere stateside, then made arrangements to have it shipped from Seattle, North to Ketchikan, via The Alaska Steamship Co. Upon his arrival in Ketchikan, the donkey was then destined to make the trip onward to Craig via the Mail Boat, named Discoverer.

This was all well and good except for one thing. The mail boat made the trip from Ketchikan to Craig, but once a week, on Monday. Bailey therefore, was confronted with a big, big problem. Because of the fact that the steamer from Seattle arrived in Ketchikan on Tuesday, Bailey was stuck with the problem of what to do about the donkey when it landed in Ketchikan one day too late to make the mail boat bound for Craig, that week.

Bailey was forced to call on his good friend Bob Ellis, who was the owner of Ellis Airlines in Ketchikan, to inquire if he knew of anyone who could care for the donkey during the interim until the mail boats return. Most fortunately for Bailey, Bob condescended to care for the donkey until mail boat time, since he had a small shed available that would serve the purpose just fine.

So far, so good. Apparently everything must have gone all right, because the mail boat showed up in Craig the following Saturday afternoon carrying a very unusual hunk of cargo destined for one, Bailey Sandifer. One would think from the amount of attention this lil' critter commanded, it must have been one of the sacred animals mentioned in the bible. When the mail boat pulled in to the dock, the whole town had turned out to see it, especially the kids. Actually, the majority of them had never actually seen any real animals, outside of a cat or dog since TV had not been introduced into S.E. Alaska at this period in time. Thus the opportunity to see Bailey's ass, first hand, created quite a stir for this little town of Craig.

Fortunately for all, the donkey was of an even temperament as all the kids were eager to touch and pet him, some so shyly it was a wonder they even made contact. However, the donkey lavished in the attention bestowed on him, displaying remarkable patience in spite of being fondled and cuddled by old and young alike. I glanced over at Bailey, and I've never witnessed a broader grin on anyone's face, not even on a circus clown, because Bailey was actually grinning from ear to ear, whereas clowns merely paint it on.

Everything went well, with the donkey following obediently as Bailey led him over the hill towards home with half the town making a parade of it, stretching out behind the donkey for a good half-mile.

Fortunately the whole entourage arrived at Bailey's house without incident although several dogs along the route lost their rabid bird brain minds over the size of the new dog in town.

During the interim before the donkey's arrival, Bailey had fenced his entire yard so that when his new conquest showed up it would be free to roam at will rather than have to be restrained in any way. Frances, Sandy's wife, was unaware that the burro had been deposited in her back yard so unfortunately was totally unprepared for the, welcome greeting, she received from her new pet.

The very first thing the donkey did upon being released was to sashay up and under her kitchen window, no doubt thinking, "This is where the carrots hang out." When Frances stuck her head out the window to investigate the cause of all the ruckus, he begged for a carrot in his own inimitable way. He layed back his ears, pointed his muzzle windowward, then raised his voice in song, venting forth with a thunderous greeting for his new mistress, "Whaaa, eeeh. haaa, haa, ha", causing poor Frances to bolt backwards, knocking over nearly everything in the kitchen.

Of course Bailey ran into the house to see if she was all right, when in spotting Frances plopped flat on the floor on her donkey, inquired, "What happened, Hon? You all right?"

Frances for once lost her cool as she bellered nearly as loud as her new pet(?). "Why didn't you tell me you brought your stupid Jackass home? Dammit, he scared me half to death." This moved Bailey to help her to her feet, then to gather her into his scrawny old arms while singing her praises. "Franny." He cooed, "You just solved my dilemma. Heck sakes, I been scratchin my brain for weeks tryin ta pick out a name for him." DAMMIT! That's it, from now on his name will be Dammit. "Thank ya, Franny, thank ya." And that's what Dammit was called from that day on.

Incidentally, Dammit proved to be very adept in hauling the oil drums over the hill in a seemingly effortless manner, while at the same time becoming the town's main attraction. He never had to make a haul alone. There was always a group of admirers more than willing to accompany him.

Heehaw, no one ever accompanied me, dammit.

SPRING MEANS SALMON

After having worked the entire winter as a handyman, I felt that I had fulfilled my obligation to the town of Craig, and therefore decided to set my sights on attaining a higher standard for myself. Spring had relentlessly pushed her way to the fore, forcing Old Man Winter to take a back seat. I had heard that the advent of spring was also that time of the year when Libbys would be taking on extra help in reactivating their cannery for the upcoming salmon season.

The townsfolk assured me that I would stand a good chance of being hired for their pre-season work since it was their policy to hire local residents on a priority basis. Sure enough, their prophecy came true and I was put to work within the following week.

Perhaps some of you are not aware that prior to Alaska's adopting statehood in 1959, fish traps were being used by the larger operators as their primary means for the taking of salmon here in Alaska. They were finally outlawed after it was discovered the traps were responsible for depleting the fish runs at a rate that was unacceptable for the survival of the salmon.

Incidentally, at this period in time a major portion of Libby's pre-season work actually involved overhauling these same fish traps. You must understand that they were huge contraptions, similar to a horse corral, except that they were four to five times larger than, but were also set out in the water. They were outfitted with the same type of leads employed in guiding cattle into a corral, and contained several individual storage areas within the trap itself, each designed to hold several thousand salmon at a time. This method of taking salmon was highly effective in intercepting and commandeering a run of fish and why not? The traps were strategically set up directly in the migratory path the salmon followed to their parent stream on their way to spawn. Following the time when a trap became reasonably full, a huge barge was sent from the packing plant, accompanied by a brailing crew who would brail the fish onto the barge, then haul them into the cannery.

We're back to pre-season work, now. Isn't all this, something?

It took a lot of work and know-how to reconstruct these garganteous fish traps since they had been stripped and beached after the end of each canning period. Now, if you don't believe me that it was one mucho biggo task pounding thousands of overly large staples into what seemed like a hundred miles of huge spruce logs, c'mon over here and grab a hammer yourself, my friend.

It took tons of special stainless steel chicken wire for each trap, and there were two of them. It was an amazing sight to see a huge barge pull into the dock, piled miles high with roll after roll of chicken wire. My first thought was, "What in Hell" I wouldn't dream they were going to can chickens, and soon found out this was an erroneous theory after having pounded eleventy five hundred pounds of staples into the spruce logs where the wire was hung. These huge barges that were later put to use to haul the fish from the traps, also required a great deal of preparation.

First off, they were run up on the grid, where once they were scraped clean, a liberal application of red scow paint was applied to the exterior portions of the barges. Bear in mind, these barges were huge, huge monstrosities, requiring not just gallons of paint, but literally hundreds of gallons of the stuff. You undoubtedly have heard of the Indian being called the Redskin. We lived up to the name very well, because that is exactly what we looked like by the time we finished slopping all this paint onto those massive hulls.

Following the paint job, the decks were given special attention to make certain they were both clean and sanitary. This was accomplished by first, painstakingly removing the old caulking in the deck seams, then re-caulking them with new cotton. Following this procedure, hot tar was then poured into all the seams. Finally to assure a clean and sanitary finish, the whole surface of the decks were swabbed thoroughly with linseed oil, making them waterproof, but also to act as a guarantee that no fish slime or other foreign matter should enter the seams to contaminate the fish.

These major tasks were assigned to the beach gang where I was sent to work. We were kept plenty busy from here on in until canning time, believe me.

The pre-season period seemed to simply gallop by, and before we knew it, the machinist crews from stateside had arrived. Their job was to make certain the canning machinery was to be in flawless condition in order that there would be no stoppages, once they started to process the salmon.

It was a strange new world in a way but highly interesting as I came to realize the scope of this pre-season operation, but I also understood why. In view of the fact that Libby's had to advance wages for 75 to 80 workers, plus feed them, and in addition to that, fork over the dough for all the equipment necessary to the operation. Whoooeee! I'd have hated to provide the cash outlay for this one.

They were gambling that the salmon pack would be sufficiently large enough for them to recoup their investment, coupled with a margin of profit.

Here comes the fun part, folks. It had been more than a month and a half, lemme see, that's like six weeks ago when the work had begun. Now lo and behold, the first load of salmon has arrived at the cannery for processing. Holy yumped up yimminy, what a thrilling sight to see not hundreds, but rather thousands of salmon pouring into the holding bins all sorted and ready to be processed the following day according to their species. Following a pattern, the (humpies) pink salmon, were generally processed first, due to the fact they were more predominant in S. E, Alaska than the (silvers)Coho, (ketah)dog salmon, or the (sockeye)reds.

I was stationed at the receiving end of the fish elevator where the barges loaded with salmon, delivered their cargo. I was aghast in seeing a barge pull up to the elevator carrying something like 25,000 fish amassed in one heaping mountain of shiny, beautiful salmon. However, by the end of the day I was literally ungassed, because one other beach gang member other than myself, his name was George Edenso, Jr., was obliged to push the mountain of fish from the barge, onto the elevator. Did I ever learn in a hurry to push the fish from the high side of the load, toward the front, because heaven help you if you let the load tilt back; "From there on in brother." You were compelled to push every one of those blankety blank, beautiful salmon, up hill.

A STROKE OF LUCK. The following day things took a turn for the better, as one of the machinist helpers had to go stateside because of illness. I was called upon to take his place. This was quite a step upwards for me, not only in a monetary sense, but prestige-wise as well. The whole canning operation was dependent entirely on the machinist crew to keep the machines in perfect running order, so consequently they were given the distinction of being A-Okay!

It was but a short time later that another one of the machinists quit the cannery. Once again I was called upon to take his place, sorta catapulting from a helper, into a machinists rating. Thank goodness this position was not so technical as some of those the other machinists held. However, and I am not inclined to brag, I did handle my new assignment very well, and because of this I was granted a permanent position as a machinist in Libby's future operations. My ability to fill in like this actually played a substantial part in my receiving another job offer from Libby's.

There was a rumble making the rounds throughout the Territory, or perhaps it was preempted knowledge that Alaska would without a doubt, be seeking Statehood within the foreseeable future. The Bureau of Indian Affairs had already devised a strategy for the natives of Alaska which would enable them to become self sufficient, rather than remain wards of the Government as was their present tenure. The program was designed for the purpose of guaranteeing employment, equal opportunity, and financial success to all the native villages throughout Southeastern, Alaska. To put it bluntly, the Bureau intended to cause the Indians to become an integral part of the Salmon industry, launching them into competition with Libby McNeill, and Libby here in Craig. Washington Fish and Oyster Co who was operating out of Ketchikan, and also The Nackett Packing of Waterfall, which incidentally, was owned by The Atlantic and Pacific Tea Co. All those who were reaping the profits, but not necessarily planting the crop. This is when my latest job offer came about.

The Bureau of Indian Affairs had compiled an agreement with Libby's to rebuild an old abandoned cannery in the town of Klawock. Klawock was a true native village, with a population of 150 inhabitants, who by a majority were Thlinget Indians, outside of a Presbyterian Minister and his wife, - - Ross and Sylvia Cleeland.

Libby's had agreed to reconstruct the dilapidated structure to the point where it was functional. After this was accomplished, they were to oversee the operation in behalf of the Bureau of Indian Affairs for a period covering three full years, with the stipulation that

Libby's shall be entitled to whatever profits they might glean during the designated time. However, it was also agreed that Libby's must instruct the natives in the management, the selling, and the actual operation of the cannery so that theoretically, within three years time the Indians would then be capable of becoming self-supporting by operating the cannery themselves, should Alaska actually become a State.

This is when good fortune came booming into the picture in my behalf.

One afternoon my Superintendent approached me to ask if I would consider making a move from Craig to Klawock to become caretaker for Libby's interests, and properties? The deal was to include a house to live in, all my fuel supplied, free electricity, plus a salary equivalent to the amount I was being paid in Craig? "Sure." That's all I had to say, leaving him with the impression that I was a truly devoted employee. One who was willing to make sacrifices for the good of the company, when in reality I was singing at the top of my lungs within my perfectly conditioned, muscular and attractive body. Oops, sorry, kinda got carried away there.

DAMMIT AGAIN

It was no longer than a month or so after Dammit had taken Craig by storm, when Bailey received a package from Ellis Air marked C.O.D., in the amount of $26.75. He pondered over a large "Partial Shipment" notice stamped on the outside of the package, figuring they were probably returning some of the tack that had been left with Dammit at the time they were caring for him in Ketchikan.

Nevertheless, he paid the billing in order to receive the package, all the while turning and shaking it in an endeavor to determine "What in hell!" it contained, as he put it. The thing that had him really baffled was another other sticker on the opposite side, which read, "PERISHABLE", in large bold letters.

Bailey went chop, chop home, anxious to uncover what was in the package, only to open it and find, and this is no B.S my friends, a whole cartonful of road apples. Bob was kind enough to explain, "Hey old buddy, I'm sorry I was so negligent in not having sent all of Dammit to you as promised, so please accept this shipment in good faith as the remains of what was due, you. Please, no need for a thank you, after all, what are friends for?

Bailey, the old devil, affixed upon me the most Angelic smile he could muster as he pompously and in a highly dignified manner marched out the door with his precious package clutched tightly to his bony old chest. He then ceremoniously knelt down to painstakingly deposit several road apples at the base of each of his rose bushes. After having completed this arduous task, he laboriously arose, then with head held high, took his final curtain by announcing, "As you can see,

I've always fed my plants the very finest and most expensive fertilizer money can buy. It was most difficult for me to hold my tongue but I was actually thinking, "Ya danged ol' coot! I think you're the one who's fulla fertilizer."

Bob Ellis was very fond of Yane, (the Indian name for sea cucumber). I don't know if anyone of you might be familiar with this huge sea slug. They actually resemble a snail that has been decked out with a whole series of stubby tentacles covering its entire body. You're bound to think, "Uuugh," in seeing one but do not let their appearance fool you. They are mouthwateringly delicious, having a flavor equivalent to or even tastier than a razor clam. I'm talking about a razor clam that has been expertly prepared. One that after having acquired a wonderfully crisp and succulent golden brown texture, requires that you quickly chomp down with the old bicuspids, masticate, then swallow. Mmmm! A Yane is like that! Incidentally, the commercial name for Yane is Trepang! They sell for like twelve bucks a pound in New York if you're able to find them.

Bob Ellis is so fond of Yane he flies over here quite frequently in his private plane for no other reason than to go Yane Pickin as it is called here in S.E. Alaska. I'm trying to decide if Bob singularly flew in for Yane this time, or did he really fly over to make amends to Sandy for his odorous conduct. (Here we go using that name again) Bob has always called Bailey, Sandy, so we're not calling Bailey, Bailey at this particular time.

Well now, the Yane pickin went off smooth asglass due to the fact they had commandeered their old Thlinget Indian friend Billy Chuck, to go along with them. Billy simply stood upon the pontoons of the plane Bob had flown, whereas all he had to do was guide him through a shallow grassy area, signaling which direction he wished for him to taxi, thus enabling him to pick up the Yane with the greatest of ease. When they felt they had picked enough sea cucumbers, Bob simply flew Sandy and Billy back to Craig. With his Yane in a bucket, and no doubt having himself a good laugh while reminiscing over the Dammit incident, good ol' Bob pointed the nose of his plane homeward and flew off into the sunset making it an ideal ending for an ideal day. (aint that nice)

G'BYE CRAIG - - - HELLO KLAWOCK

Hey there, fellow travelers:

I truly hope you've enjoyed your Alaska venture up to this point, and that I've enabled you to have experienced both physical and spiritual change, as you view this beautiful virgin land. As I promised, have you not shared in an ever-changing variable to your normal life style. Ha! ya ain't seen nothing yet! We're leaving Craig behind as we venture forth to live in a third world native village. Cars, sirens, and other people's affairs shall take a back seat to every day adventures that are nothing more than routine living to the Thlinget Indians here in Klawock.

Klawock proved to be a small village of no more than 150 inhabitants, the majority of whom were true Thlinget Indians. It took the greater part of a year before we gained the confidence of the natives in order for them to accept my wife and I on friendly terms. Even then there were a few die-hards who were reluctant to accept whites living in their village, but fortunately it boiled down to a very few, so we felt comfortable with that. However, after we were finally accepted into the village, we were treated royally and became equally as fond of our Indian friends as they grew fond of us. Actually, I do not choose to describe them as Indian friends. I would much rather simply say friends, because both my wife and I felt no distinction between them and ourselves.

After a period of time the Mrs. and I became more and more involved with our life in the village until eventually we found ourselves intensely involved in their community activities, which also included weddings and funerals, as well as a number of social events.

We both sang in the choir at Christmas time and also at Easter time when the natives put on the neatest cantatas. The Indians are gifted with beautiful singing voices, but my wife was by far the most outstanding member of the choir during the presentation of these cantatas.

It so happened that Roy Peratrovich, a high ranking officer from Juneau who was connected with the Bureau of Indian Affairs located in Juneau, arrived as a guest in our village right at Christmas time and so quite naturally, was invited to attended the rendition of our Christmas music. Unaware that my wife and I had become permanent residents in Klawock, and upon espying her in the choir loft, inquired, "Who's that little blonde with all the blackheads?" This created an uproarious burst of laughter and a lot of kidding about my wife and her blackheads. However, this incident does serve to substantiate the claim that my wife was by far the most outstanding member of the choir, because we also presented these same Cantatas to the neighboring towns of Craig and Haidaburg, where everyone immediately sought to single out the blonde with all the blackheads.

SOCIAL STATUS

As in almost every small town, there is always an underlying current from one faction or the other that is seeking to become more influential than the other in regards to political issues and community functions. The same holds true in our little town of Klawock. This is actually a good thing, because it keeps everything in balance. You must have pro's and con's in order to function as a community.

How fortunate for this village that it had two Senators from Alaska actually living in Klawock. Men who kept abreast of current happenings, and who were also knowledgeable in the operation of city government.

The Peratrovich family carried a lot of weight throughout the village through one of several brothers, a Democratic Senator by the name of Frank Peratrovich. Frank was the proprietor of a grocery store, along with his wife Hattie here in Klawock during the times when the Senate was not in session. Jim Peratrovich was the oldest male in the family, one who was very strict and set in the old Indian way, and one who would not accept change. He was adamant in his efforts to influence the young people in the village to hold onto the old Indian traditions. Frank on the other hand was very liberal and understanding, one who continuously strived to improve conditions for the Alaska Natives in issues pertaining to education, or any other issues leading towards the advancement of his people.

I am not totally certain as to the actual relationship of the other Peratrovich males to one another, but I shall nevertheless include their names in the event it may bring back memories for those who are Thlingets and may be reading this book. Ed Peratrovich was a jewel of a man who at one time served as the mayor of the town. His wife was named Ruby, she served as our post-mistress for a number of years as did Edna Peratrovich who's husband was John Peratrovich, a local fisherman. One other brother, who went under the name of Roy, was an officer in the Bureau of Indian Affairs located in Juneau, Alaska's Capitol. Roy frequented the village very rarely, as he was preoccupied with working in Juneau.

Nonetheless, he was in a position to be very influential in issues pertaining to the betterment of the Thlinget Nation. I was aware of only two sisters related to the Peratrovich clan, one who was named Jennie Lund, a sister to Frank, and also one other who was named Roseanne Elmore. Roseanne was gifted with the abi0lity to speak the Thlinget tongue fluently, but was equally affluent in English, as well. Therefore, she became the official interpreter, acting as a go-between during meetings involving the Bureau of Indian Affairs, City Council meetings, or Tribal Council meetings.

No matter if they were social functions, weddings, banquets or whatever, there was Roseanne. I marveled at her ability to understand those speaking in the Thlinget tongue, and then convert it into English with hardly a pause. This guttural gibberish stuff was flying at her as swiftly as a swallow darts for bugs, while she just stood quietly describing that the sky was blue, the vote was cast, or the mayor never wore shorts, whatever. I was utterly amazed that she could translate any one of the speakers guttural narrations with the same rapidity as it was being presented.

I recall mentioning there was another family residing in Klawock equally as influential as the Peratrovich family, who went by the name of Demmert. Their sons excelled in teaching and in music, while the parents were very strong leaders in Indian culture. Three of the five Demmert brothers went Stateside to earn their degrees in education then returned to their native towns to continue in the teaching field. Art Demmert was a talented pianist and I marveled at his ability to keep the keys individually separated as he played, because if a Walrus had hands, that would be how large Art's hands were. His younger brother Larry, was adept in conducting, therefore it was he who conducted both the Easter and Christmas cantatas for the local choir. Art played the piano that provided the music for the cantatas, so the cantatas proved to be truly a work of Art.

Everyone called her Mamma Demmert, but her real name was SuhKwa! She spoke no English, while her husband, Papa George, spoke both English and Thlinget. At town meetings or social gatherings, Mamma Demmert was inevitably called upon to speak to the elder element, the majority of whom, also, could speak no English. I recognized her repeated use of the words, (Khon Khahu?) She was asking them to believe in God, to be honest and caring for one another, things of this nature. She was the kindest and most knowledgeable Indian lady we've ever met. In addition to this, by conferring with her sons, she always made certain all those present were led to understand everything that was going on. Quite naturally she was highly influential with the elders of the tribe because of her ability to relate.

The Demmerts were, all of them, a really exceptional family in that they consistently portrayed a kindly and friendly attitude, along with a sincere willingness to aid others, which in itself is a remarkable attribute considering the fact that the average native is not that obligatory toward his fellow man.

The Demmerts just like the Peratrovichs, were also privileged to boast of a Senator on their side of the family in the person of Al Widmark who was a Republican Senator, and also ran a grocery store in Klawock whenever his Congress was not in session. His wife's name was Carmel, who I believe was a sister to Charlie Demmert, an uncle to the Demmerts already mentioned in the story, and might I add, a true Alaska Legend in himself if ever there was one. I've expounded on his many diversified accomplishments farther on in the book, so I will not offer a dissertation on him at this particular time.

In spite of there being two power factors in our little town, City Government ran smoothly due to the mutual cooperation of these two Senators whose primary interests were to do their best for their people.

FOOD - - APLENTY

You'll probably be drooling down your fronts while I describe to you all the yummy foods available to you in this magic land, Alaska.

Prior to adopting Statehood, and prior to McDonalds, Whataburger or Bank One, living off the land was actually a reality rather than a fable.

Ask yourself this question. What does man require to sustain life? Along with water he requires meat, veggies, and fruit. We got lots of that stuff up here in Alaska. All you have to know is how to utilize it.

So in place of beef, the natives would oft times substitute bear meat. Surprisingly when a bear first comes out of hibernation and has not yet developed a set of Charles Atlas muscles, the meat resembles beef, both in texture and in flavor.

Our deer farms encompassed all the many islands relative to Southeast Alaska. Understand that during the worst part of winter as we cruised the islands, we made sure we carried an axe or chain saw in order to fell a number of cedars, which then became forage for the groups of deer that were inhabiting the islands. In other words, we were actually throwing bales of hay to our cattle just as the ranchers do stateside.

Of course, our greatest source of meat was nice fresh seafood. The area immediately surrounding Klawock abounded in several species of trout, salmon, halibut and crab.

There was an abundance of all kinds of funny stuff that was quite edible, but I can't claim they were yummy. Lady slippers and abalone were great. Gum boots were like rubber bootheels. I could not for the life of me understand why the natives would even attempt to eat them unless it was to wile away a whole day in an endeavor to masticate the damn thing to the point where one might swallow it without choking to death.

The Thlingets were prone to using seaweed even more than we used lettuce. After it is dried then pulverized, it is sprinkled over most any dish to enhance the flavor, especially, in my opinion, when it's a combination of fish and rice. Thus seaweed is actually an ideal supplement to the scarcity of green stuff.

Folks, I'm afraid I could go on and on forever over all the food available from these waters, but you're bound to find out eventually, so I'll simply dog it off and give you a breather, okay?

Damn it all, I can't contain myself. I just gotta mention clams, lingcod, red snapper, etc, etc, etc. Maybe in another chapter I could tell you about cranberries, salmon berries, rhubarb, and goose tongue.

Have I mentioned ducks? Geese? - - - ?

CLAMMING – BUT DOING IT RIGHT

The most enjoyable part of your joining up with me in Klawock shall come about through your getting acquainted with the Woods family.

George Woods and his wife, who they called Liz, raised three of the most wonderful guys anyone could wish to become interconnected with. There were three brothers, Bill, Frank, and Leo, who were all three near my age which enhanced our chances for establishing a companionable relationship, and it did blossom into just that.

These three brothers literally took it upon themselves to teach me to hunt and to take care of myself in this wilderness that was then Alaska. They taught me their customs, their beliefs, what local food was edible, and even how to prepare it. They instructed me in how to find it, while at the same time taught me how to attain it. There was no end to the effort they put forth in my behalf in order that I know the land as they did, and so enable me to fall in love with the primitive way of life that was essential at this period in time, prior to Alaska's accepting Statehood.

Nearly all of the incidents brought forth in this book, we invited of our own volition. On the other hand, a good percentage of the uninvited incidents being brought forth as this book is being written, are those that were part of the sharing and caring on their parts, to make sure I should become a good Indian. So come along with us and you, too, shall become good Indians.

The Woods boys owned a forty-foot seine boat named the Harry, Jr., which they used time and time again to venture forth in search of fish and game. However, they were not above seeking out any of the other numerous goodies native to the area, should they show up while we were out cruising. Each and every time the boys were preparing to go on an expedition to hunt, dig clams, or go fishing, whatever the occasion, they offered me a berth on the Harry, Jr. All I had to do was grab a sleeping bag, jump aboard, and we were off on a trip that would set some of the would-be sportsmen from Stateside back one big wad of bucks. For instance, the awesome beauty of a sunrise like the one I am about to describe would well be worth a big part of that wad of dough, even though they hadn't roped a single clam.

It is nearing 5:00 A.M, with daylight striving to enter the morn through a cottony mass of puffy white clouds resting serenely on the calmest of waters imaginable. The Harry, Jr. resembles a ghost ship coming out of nowhere with nothing more than her bow protruding through the puffy looking mass of clouds. She appears to be three stories high, due to a mystical illusion effected by the fog bank concealing her, until she emerges in her entirety with a power skiff in tow at her stern. An absolutely awesome, never to be duplicated, picturesque composition. (Holy smokes, I can't believe I wrote that. Here I am 84 yrs old, did only high school, and flunked three times. Now I ask you, wasn't that descriptive?)

Okay, before I get carried away with myself, let me enlighten you on the subject of power skiffs. Normally a skiff would be rowed by hand, while a power skiff boasts of having a 25-40 h.p.motor and is also equipped with a set of skags. The power skiff is an integral part of a seining operation. Very quickly following the moment the mother ship makes a set, (runs her seine off the stern) the power skiff tows one end of the seine, and as quickly as possible, circles the school of salmon, then returns to the parent vessel, hopefully to wrap up the school of fish. Skags are elongated wedges permanently attached to the underside of the hull at the stern. Their primary purpose is to enable the power skiff to run close to shore without suffering damage to the prop and rudder as the skiff goes shallow in pursuit of the salmon.

Now let us continue with the guys stateside paying big bucks for the trip that I am about to describe. At this point in time, the Harry, Jr. has already docked and we've all clamored aboard. We have been advised that this is to be a combination trip. First of all we will be going clamming since we are anticipating a prevailing minus tide. As soon as the tide starts back we will abandon our clamming operations or drown so in weighing our options, we've opted to go deer hunting rather than drown. It has been pounded into our cheechako brains time and time again. BE PREPARED!

I have no problem with that, so along with my trusty 30-30, I have provided myself with the very best claming gear known to man, and this consisted of a shiny new clam rake, leak-proof hip boots, and a gunny sack for packing out the clams. During the interim while the Harry, Jr. is anchoring up we were instructed to place a large wash tub in the bottom of our power skiff.

Bill was the designated skipper during this outing so consequently, and without question, we all took orders from him. Incidentally, he was the oldest of the three brothers. "Okay, into the skiff, everybody," was the command. I made a grab for my snazzy hip-boots, figuring to put them on as we headed for the gravel bar, when Bill with no more expression than a totem, informed me in a very brusque manner. "You don't need that one!" I dropped the boots rather gingerly. I made a stab for my shiny clam rake and met up with the same gruff command, "You don't need that one!" The guys always enjoyed taking me along mainly because I was so damn dumb in their Indian ways. I can tell you one thing brother, I most assuredly learned to do exactly as they said without batting an eye. However, I'm sure I detected Bill batting his eye, causing me to feel that maybe they were funning me again.

Thus, with one final attempt to be useful I sorta slunk toward the gunnysack, though never taking my eyes off of Bill. Even before he had the opportunity to "Ahem," let me have it, I dropped the lousy sack and jumped into the skiff. It for sure didn't seem likely they would have made this long run without being serious about going clamming because I knew they had brought me along for one of their endless lessons, but just the same they really had me guessing as to what was coming next. Everything was in readiness as we headed for a gravel bar protruding above the water because of the low tide. Leo was piloting the power skiff on this leg of the venture and proceeded to run her bow right up onto the gravel bar, ordering Frank and I to scamper ashore and run out an anchor apiece.

As soon as this was done, and to my utter amazement, Leo abruptly yanked the skiff around and headed away from the gravel bar causing the anchors to become firmly imbedded in the gravel while Leo kept churning with the prop. Surprisingly, all we had to do was simply stand in the prop wash and harvest whole bunches of fat little butter clams. They were hardly larger than a silver dollar, and one could detect a ring of pink flesh protruding from around the shell because the clams were so fat they couldn't close completely.

From this point we simply tossed them into the wash tub that had been deposited in the bottom of the skiff. Frank, in the meantime, had scooped up a bucket or two of sea water to throw into the tub before he added a few handfuls of raw cornmeal, explaining as he did so, "The clams are gonna eat the corn meal and spit out the sand. When you eat the clams they don't have any sand now, just corn meal." "Yank the anchors and head for the boat," Leo ordered. The clamming was completed in that short period of time.

Phillip Kudhay, one other member of our party had remained aboard the Harry, Jr. When we returned with our mess of clams, he had already prepared a huge pot of boiling water, so all we had to do was dump those tender li'l ol' bi-valves into the boiling water, then as soon as their shells popped open they were considered done. Phillip had already melted a half pound of butter, filling two dishes with the golden brown aromatic liquid, so as we dragged a clam from the boiling water, we simply swiped it through the butter, then seagull-like, gulped it down, heads, tails, feathers and all.

Mmm, mmm, mmm were they ever good! So help me, I'll never enjoy a batch of clams more than I did those. Wow! What a way to go. Is it any wonder that people find Alaska to be so excitingly enchanting?

A GENUINE TASTE OF BUCK FEVER

After having feasted royally on that luscious batch of clams, we picked up and headed for Nahsuk to do some deer hunting. Nahsuk means wolf island in the Thlinget tongue. Since Nahsuk is one of the largest islands within our area it was noted for harboring fairly large groups of deer, and for this reason was quite frequently visited by the Thlingets in their search of game. The Thlinget hunters were also fully aware that Nahsuk was home base to a number of wolf packs.

The wolves normally travel from twenty five to fifty miles in one given direction, foraging for birds, bunny hoppers or deer, whatever the land has to offer. They commonly mark their travels by lifting their legs on various rocks, trees, or bushes along their way. Should they detect a strange scent, they would be forewarned of another pack invading the area. If the pack felt they were being intruded upon, the end result would be one vicious, hair-raising fight over territorial jurisdiction. On the other hand, if they felt they were not being crowded for space, unbelievably, they simply condescended to co-exist.

Our first step was to make sure we anchored the Harry, Jr. securely. Following this necessity, we lightered ashore in the power skiff. After securing the power skiff to the beach, we set our sights upon bagging one of those nice big bucks known to frequent this particular area. After setting me ashore, I was instructed to follow that well-defined deer trail over yonder. "Stay within sight of that trail and you can't get lost," I was warned. Ugh! What a mind-boggling thought. Get lost on Wolf Island, no thanks!

Meanwhile, the boys departed to do their own thing while I dutifully followed the deer trail as instructed. After having penetrated the forest but a short distance, I commenced thinking about wolves. Since I had never been exposed to a wilderness situation prior to this moment in my life, it was but a simple matter for me to conjure up all kinds of spooky things in my mind's' eye. It soon developed that I became cognizant of a new and frightening experience, and that was to discover how relentlessly aloneness can creep up on you. Bit by bit it eats at you, as you become more aware that you are, as of now, completely and totally a-l-o-n-e, maybe with wolves. Boy oh boy, do you ever long for the companionship of a buddy at this particular moment.

Bullldozer-like, this eerie feeling encompasses your whole being, your skin does the creepies, while every bush around you appears to take on an image of something life threatening. Soon after you reach this plain of psychic dilemma, it actually gets worse. Unbelievable as it may seem, you must face the fact that as of now you are in a world void of sound. It's really weird, but the silence itself comes crashing in around you, forcing you to feel the grim reaper might at any time become your sole companion. It is a singularly awesome feeling that no man can portray unto you. Instead you are compelled to withstand this challenge entirely on your own.

Just as sure as fate, no more had I thought about it, when it happened, After having proceeded along the designated trail for perhaps 200 yds I came upon a steep rise. Struggling up the incline, huffing and puffing, robbed me of my concentration so by the time I had reached the top of the rise something else had reached the top of the rise, only from the opposite side. I immediately detected something gray. I froze in terror knowing for sure it was a wolf, but to my utter disbelief there stood a huge buck staring me in the face, eye to eye.

We stood facing each other for at least an hour and fifteen minutes, peering deep into each other's eyes. Okay, so maybe it was a minute and fifteen seconds, but believe me it seemed like the longer period of time. All the time I was thinking, my gawd what an awesome situation. I had never in my life been this close to a buck and here we are in the middle of a wilderness with only the two of us being present. Before I had time to think any more thoughts, this beautiful animal turned and with a single bound, left me gasping for breath with my heart doing rhythms a heart was never designed to do, as he wheeled and rocketed off into the underbrush nearby.

I wasn't even aware of my rifle in my hands until I stumbled over the damn thing. Needless to say, I got educated for real, once more. I learned what Buck Fever was all about as I retraced my steps back to the Harry, Jr. without a trace of fear that a wolf might appear.

What a relief for my pounding heart to discover the boys were back after having bagged game, so we headed homeward for Klawock to await another trip and perhaps a trophy. I didn't dare say a thing to the boys about my trophy, but to this day I can readily visualize the sight of that splendid animal towering above me. Also, in any given moment I can recall the rush I felt as he stared straight into my eyes, not actually showing fear as much as curiosity before he wheeled, severing contact with me and was gone.

As they say, "Gone but not forgotten," beautiful wild creature. Most assuredly not forgotten, and thank you so much for not having been a wolf.

DAHKEENOO-EASTER

In my estimation, this trip will top them all. It ranks as one of the most educational as well as the most adventurous undertaking you'll be subjected to, bar none, so grab a pair of tennis shoes and let's go.
 The Harry, Jr. is fast approaching the float. Hey, no whimpering. I know it's barely 5:00 A. M., but that's how it's done up here. Actually you should be focusing on the beauty of the morning. Daylight is already worming its way into full bloom, with a smattering of stars stubbornly holding on in their struggle to maintain their dominant position in the night sky.
 Hop aboard, our boat has docked with Frank, Bill, and Leo on deck. May I introduce you to Phillip Khuday, who quite frequently accompanies us in the capacity of cook. Phillip is our fun guy who is always good for a laugh or two, (shares some of the booboos with me). In the event that someone within earshot utters a derogatory remark of some kind, Phillip immediately picks up on it and is quick to respond with, "Hey, watch it, I resemble that remark," which throws him into a fit of laughter like he said something that really cracked us up. Oh well!
 `We were warned in advance that this trip was to be a real fun one, making it compulsory that we wear our tenny runners, (Thlinget way of describing tennis shoes), since we were to encounter some rather tricky climbing.
 I had no idea what lay ahead at this time, darnn guys, they always wanted to keep me guessing. It wasn't until we were well under way that we were informed; the purpose of this trip is to gather Easter eggs. Oh sure! I immediately assumed they were fun-

nin me again. It turned out we were heading for DahKeeNoo Island, an Indian name referring to, "The Island With a Fort," so called because at one time during World War II there had been a gun emplacement there in the event of a Japanese invasion. DahKeeNoo turned out to be a massive monolith having no beach line and with nothing but sheer rock cliffs showing at the waters edge as it sat facing the open ocean. This allowed for huge swells to encompass its perimeter, swells that continually charged forth to create a resounding burst of spray. It was a breathtakingly, beautiful sight until we realized, for criminy sakes, don't tell us this is where the Woods boys are contemplating taking us to gather eggs?

Let's face it, it's true. This is where they plan to go about the business of gathering Murry bird eggs, which the Thlingets substituted for Easter eggs.

The Murre is a small diving bird, much the same size as a small duck. They, along with other sea birds, had elected to adopt this massive rock formation as their breeding and nesting grounds.

At this point in time the Harry, Jr. has found a sheltered cove some distance away from where we will be making our attempt to gain access to the rock. Wheee! It's kinda fun riding the swells in the power skiff as we approach the monolith in order to survey the waves booming into it's massive bulk. Apparently we're gonna hafta scamper onto that part of the rock facing the ocean where the prevailing winds from the West give the ocean swells an additional boost as they too, make an attempt to climb it's face.

The boys have finally decided on a likely spot so have nosed the skiff straight in towards their target. You know, riding a huge roller coaster, diving for pearls or chasing shoats, none of these things can compare in excitement with what is about to happen next.

Phillip Khuday is offering me encouragement. "Okay, John, watch close. The trick is to jump from the skiff to the rock the same time the wave brings you in, "That's how you gonna do it, okay?" Wait a cotton pickin minute. You guys forgetting I'm a Cheechako? Maybe I don't wanna become an Indian. How come you guys don't raise chickens for your Easter eggs? I keep forgetting, chickens don't have enough hair on their legs to withstand winter. All kinds of brilliant thoughts are flashing through my mind at this time. Man, they're expecting me to jump from this heaving and surging skiff for some lousy Easter eggs. I'm wracking my brain in an effort to recall if they mentioned the eggs were of gold, now that would make this leap worth while, then it dawned on me, they were funnin me again. How dumb can you be? At the same time I'm wondering would they actually go through all this just for laughs.

Wrong! Can you believe it this is for real. Frankie has already positioned himself at the bow of the skiff steadying himself against the surge of the waves by grasping the bow line firmly, legs spread wide while leaning back hard just like a chariot rider. At the same time Bill is maneuvering the skiff into position towards the huge rock cliff. Frankie all at once makes an Olympic type leap forward grabbing at the rock, while Bill simultaneously slams into reverse just in time to avoid being bashed into the cliff from the ocean swells. It is now Leo's turn to challenge the pounding surf. Since Leo was the most athletically inclined, he made the jump perfectly.

Our fun guy Phillip, was next in line to test his prowess as a leaper, but unfortunately he did a great job of it. We were anticipating a bundle of laughs. Wanna make a guess who's turn it is now? I don't know what prompted me to tell Phillip he was a great leaper. Quite naturally he turned it around claiming I called him a Leper which afforded him the opportunity to quote his favorite quote, "Hey, I resemble that last remark", which tended to ease the tension for me to make my jump. I did quite well thank you, in view of the fact that I had four voices bellering in unison, "Jump, John, jump!"

However, I must give Bill credit for his dexterity in maneuvering the skiff away from the surging waters at precisely the right time. If it were not for his special skills that big ol' rock could have stepped in easily, for the kill.

Following a steep, steep climb up the side of the rock we were rewarded with a view that immediately caused all the stress we had so recently endured, to become non-existent. Sitting atop this monstrous monolith viewing the ocean waves far below that for some unknown reason now appeared to be puny, we lavished over the soothing ocean breeze caressing our faces, while literally thousands of sea-birds darted by, screaming their defiance at our intruding upon their sanctuary.

It is time to acknowledge that we have finally arrived at the nesting sites atop the cliffs. Wow, what a sight! Unbelievably, the nests were so numerous it was nearly impossible to avoid stepping on them. They were not actually nests but rather miniscule hollow spots in the rocks, which seemed to suffice for the sea-birds to lay theirs eggs and rear their young. We witnessed Puffins, Auklets, and Murres, and of course the ever present seagulls and Cormorants, all nesting in close proximity to one another with a total disregard for segregation of species. However, the several species of sea birds had one thing in common as each nest contained exactly four eggs.

I'm afraid I'm painting too tranquil a scene. This is chaos. The wind has commenced to blow like mad. There is in excess of eleventeenthousand angry sea birds in panicky flight, beating their stubby but stout wings close to your head, which in itself is creating a sound similar to an audience applauding the finale of, The Phantom of the Opera. On top of all that you should hear these birds voice there anger over our being here. What an earsplitting, screeching racket. There, now that takes care of the tranquility.

The boys seemed to express a preference for Murry bird eggs. Hells fire, I don't know a Murry bird from a worry bird so I'm in trouble again. Phillip was kind enough explain. "Hey Johnnie, the Murry bird got the egg what is bigger, they got the pear shape, and they got the color of gray with black blotches, brown with white blotches, greenish ones with black lines running round them, etc. Okay, you don't have to never mind the colors, okay? You gonna get the ones who are pear shaped." "Thanks a lot Phil, that helps a lot?" He was actually quite accurate, because the eggs were a variety of all the colors he described, and more.

I wondered aloud, "How in the world could any of these birds identify it's own nest when they all looked identical, especially when there were so many color combinations to contend with. By way of offering an explanation, Phillip hollered across at me. "Hey Johnnie, watch this." He bent down to remove an egg from a nest at his feet, then placed it in an adjoining nest. He then extracted an egg from that nest only to place it in the original nest from where he began his demonstration. Following this he signaled that we should step back and observe.

No sooner had we stepped back when a Murre came zooming in to land on her clutch of eggs, then immediately and all in one motion kicked the offending egg out of the nest as she settled down over the remaining three. It was but a matter of seconds before another Murre came gliding in to land on her clutch, only to repeat in one deft motion the act of kicking out the stranger in her nest the same as the other Murre had done. I was highly impressed at the birds ability to identify one grain of sand from another, so to speak. I then hurried to join up with the others who were busily selecting Murry bird eggs; an egg here, an egg there, being very careful so as to not deplete any one nest. They were quite knowledgeable in understanding that to deprive a nest of but only one egg would do no harm to the colony.

You know what? We've got enough eggs so we are now gonna get into the fun stuff. Transporting our eggs down the side of this steep, and unaccommodating mountain of rock will require skill, agility and luck, if we're to get back to where Bill is awaiting our return, hopefully with all our eggs intact.

We've all made sure our belts are good and tight since we've got the eggs stuffed inside our shirts in order to leave our hands free for the journey down the rock. Our biggest concern is that when we transfer from the rock to the power skiff, the eggs shall arrive in the proper state for boiling, rather than become a scrambled egg, Easter morning breakfast. Needless to say this phase of the operation turned out to be more challenging than doing the Olympics. Creeping downhill is a lot more hazardous than when one is facing uphill.

We've arrived. We were hoping to encounter a much milder surf when we made our jumps, but you know Ma Nature. Given the opportunity, she'll nail ya, the waves were still huge. The first two in our party to make the leap were Frankie and Leo. They were highly successful in that only two eggs were cracked. Phillip Khuday our funny guy fooled us all, he made a great leap. Only thing is, he tripped over the seats in the power skiff when Bill slammed into reverse. I'm at a loss to describe the mess he had in his lap except to say, "Damn, what a mess," whereupon he immediately countered with, "Hey, I resemble that last remark."

I timed my jump quite well considering the fact that I was a dumb Cheechako, there were so many hands reaching out to cushion my landing, plus the fact they really didn't care if I busted my butt, they just wanted to make sure we didn't sacrifice any more eggs. Their many kindnesses oft times touched my foolish heart.

All the way back to Klawock, Phillip kept us in stitches while busily extracting shells and glop from the front of his trousers, exclaiming that he thought he caught a gooeyduck but it got away, plus several other ribald remarks which I choose to leave to your imagination.

Incidentally, I'd like to mention, there were other groups from the village getting Easter eggs at the same time as us, only in a different local with which they were familiar. When they too arrived in Klawock, there was much ado involved in dispersing the eggs evenly amongst the families in preparation for their Easter activities which was the following day. When boiled, Murre eggs were treated exactly the same way as chicken eggs, the only difference being that the Murre eggs were already colored. It was the weirdest thing to discover the white part of the eggs (the albumen) was totally transparent. I was able to observe this unusual feature when on Easter morning everywhere you looked, there would be an Indian kid munching away on a Murry bird egg, no doubt captured after an intensive Easter egg hunt in Totem Park. I actually thought I was seeing things the first time I saw a child peel an egg. "How in the heck did he get the yolk out without my seeing him do it, or was it because the egg was entirely all yolk. I got up real close to the next egg peeler, so when she held the egg in her hand I could see for myself that the albumen was crystal clear, leading you to believe you were seeing things, when actually there was nothing to see, don't you see?

Nevertheless, the Murre eggs proved to be delectable, having a flavor equal to that of a nice fresh hen's egg. They also proved to be excellent for use in baking, with one exception.

My wife was thrilled to death that we had fresh eggs for a change rather than those awful cold storage eggs we were accustomed to using. This inspired her to bake a nice fresh cake for Easter that we might invite our two friends, Art and Virginia Demmert over for a game of cards, and to enjoy a serving of freshly baked cake. Our guests had arrived. We were visiting and playing cards while the cake was baking, and sending forth it's tantalizing message of something special in the wind. Our complacency was suddenly interrupted when my wife jumped up all bug-eyed, aghast that something was oozing out of the oven and onto the kitchen floor. We just couldn't imagine, "What in the world?

Arts wife volunteered that she didn't think we should put two eggs in the cake, cause the Murre eggs rise up real more than the chickens eggs, adding, "Cause when we make a cake we sometimes don't use the whole egg." "We put in half." "Sometimes we make a real big cake to use a whole egg, so we don't have to throw the other half away." "Wahsaw?" (understand) My wife responded with a rather meek kind of squeak that sounded like, "Oh!" After all what more was there to say?

However, amidst our red faces, our adeptness at cleaning up messes, and a lot of good-natured laughter, we did eventually succeed in having a very nice, cakeless Easter.

THE FAMILY TREE

At this period in time we've already spent quite a few years in Klawock. Things have advanced to the point where we have been genuinely accepted by the people of the village and are to be adopted into the tribe, which is an extremely rare honor.

In addition to, and besides hunting and fishing, we found ourselves participating in an abundance of social activities right here in the town of Klawock. Everything seemed just opposite from the way we were accustomed to conducting our lives while living Stateside. In the city we rarely knew our neighbor, while here in Klawock everyone's life seemed to touch on one another's. It worked comparable to and similar to the expression, "Birds of a Feather."

My wife and I had become close friends with Art and Virginia Demmert with whom we played cards quite frequently. If we were not at their house of an evening, they would more than likely be at ours. Suhkway, their mother, and Papa George, their father, were very influential in tribal matters and it was they who wished to adopt my wife and I into their Thlinget family. My adopted name was to be Kinduh Kut Neek, a name that indicated I belonged to the Raven Tribe. The name was taken after a constellation in the sky, Kinduh Dah Teen, proclaiming that I was a prince who was related to the dog salmon, one of their prime sources of food, therefore I was to be regarded with high esteem as a provider.

I believe my wife's adopted name was to be Kuh Khuda Khoon. (I may be mistaken as to the spelling since I'm really not too sure of this one). Her given name was intended to mean the East Wind, which would make her a very strong and influential princess, related to the Eagle tribe. During the adoption ceremonies as we were being presented with our Indian names by the elders of the village, they inadvertently offered my wife an Indian name that created quite a stir amongst the council members. Following a whole lot of gesturing, guttural chitchat and giggling, it was determined the name they were to bestow upon my wife was a no-no. It was a Raven name.

Of course, all this was being enacted in the Thlinget tongue so my wife and I had no idea what was going on. Naturally we were fearful there were complications arising that might prohibit us from being adopted into the tribe. I hadn't the vaguest notion why I was the recipient of a few slaps on the back, along with some obscene gestures from a few of the older women sitting in council, depicting, "shame on you, Johnnie".

Fortunately, Papa George came forth with an explanation for what had transpired, but at the same time kept grinning like a Cheshire Cat. "Johnnie, if you wife tooked that name, it's gonna be you married to you sister." "Better she is going to be KuhKhuda Khoon." "This is the Eagle name."

Aha! I became aware that herein lay the answer to something I had been pondering for quite some time. The question had been on my mind as to how the Indians managed to avoid interracial marriages. Now it was clear to me.

As we keep a family tree and thus avoid having cousins marrying cousins so does the Indian retain the lineage of an individual by the Indian name that individual adopts. In other words, an Eagle must marry a Raven when by the same token a Raven is compelled by tribal law to marry an Eagle. There was my answer. Very simple, but nevertheless very effective.

Our town hall in Klawock was very large and served as a center for nearly all our social activities which created a feeling of togetherness unlike anything we could have experienced in the states. Adults, teens and kids alike attended whatever activities they had to offer. The hall ministered to dances, weddings and funerals as well. In addition to this they held public meetings, graduation exercises, Indian dances, and wakes. A complete sell-out occurred whenever there was basketball competition between the neighboring towns of Craig, and Haidaburg. (Mainly because the tickets were free)

Is it any wonder that we became part of a large family? Man oh man, what a wonderful world this could be if only all people would conduct themselves in a like manner. There is so much good stuff out there if only greed and self- centeredness would vacate the scene.

The only kink in this beautiful program lies in the fact that we were forced to conduct our own funerals since we were more or less isolated from these facilities in our little town. During the years we spent in Klawock, we participated in over forty funerals due to the fact that the cannery carpenter shop was used in the preparation of the coffins. We ordered the satin material with which to line the coffins, from Ketchikan. The men in the village possessed the necessary skills to construct a really nice substitute for the real thing. The services were properly conducted by our Presbyterian minister, Reverend Ross Cleeland, who was residing at the Manse with his wife Sylvia and their two sons, Gene and Byron.

Hold it right there! Damn, I forgot to mention the most fun thing that ever occurred at the town hall. It had to do with Christmas. The natives erected a massive Christmas tree all decorated with lights and ornaments equivalent to any found in Siberia, Turkey or Yokohama. All the presents from every family in town were brought forth and deposited at the base of this massive tree.

As Christmas Eve grew near, every family in the village gathered at the Town Hall to sing Christmas

Carols. The kids put on cute little skits, as well as others who sang for the audience, or performed individually on the stage. The fun part, the primary reason for the gathering shall now come into play. It is time to release the mountain of gifts heaped high under the huge tree. Actually distributing the gifts was the best part of the evening. A dozen or so of the more popular males were elected to pass out the presents by grabbing a package from under the tree. He would then holler out that person's name as loudly as he could (quite necessary it be loud due to the festive uproar from the excited children in anticipation for their name being called.)

Stepping over and around bodies, toys, and already deflowered packages in order to locate your party was a pack of fun, both exhilarating and exciting, as well as actually becoming compounded in scope, as more wrappings, toys and people became an integral part of the beehive of activities. A clamor of voices emitting a variety of ooh's and aah's was continuously accelerating into higher levels of sound as more and more wonderful surprises became exposed. What a terrific way to celebrate Christmas Eve in comparison to just sitting and watching the boob tube.

This was such a fun happening and it truly ignited the whole village into feeling the real spirit of Christmas.

NAHSUK- - WOLF ISLAND

It is wintertime here in Klawock where we are now into the second week of February. We have returned once more to NahSuk, our favorite hunting grounds situated in a wilderness miles from nowhere, somewhere in S. E. Alaska. It is miserably cold so we have all donned rubber pants and jackets in an effort to retain our body's warmth. In addition to this there isn't a single sound to be heard, only an eerie void, as we tromp doggedly through a large muskeg in search of game.

Pardon me, I am sadly mistaken. The ring of ice encircling the bottom of my rubber pants is creating sound. It is a most disturbing swish, swish, swish sound, almost indiscernible in this weird silence, but at the same time totally distracting as we forge ahead through a stand of what the Indians call smiling berry bushes. It is in reality salal brush also coated with ice, adding its bit to the annoying, rubbing sound that could alert any game within the area of our presence. Fortunately the salal brush encircled the outer perimeter of the island so as we advanced inland we eventually departed from the ice coated brush and entered into the forest.

This venture happens to be singularly spooky in that NahSuk is the domain for several packs of wolves, who, as I mentioned previously, forage in one direction for a matter of miles, then reverse their direction to seek whatever game they might uncover on the return trip. Wolves have at certain times been observed fighting fiercely over territorial rights and should one bear witness to an encounter of this magnitude, that person shall be granted the opportunity to witness every hair on his body, arms and head, stand on end at precisely the same moment.

So here we are, a party of four made up of three brothers, Frank, Leo, Bill woods and myself. Frank and I had condescended to cover the middle section of the island. Leo had elected to hunt to the East of us, while Bill quite naturally agreed that he would cover to the West of us. We decided that everyone should proceed in a Northerly direction, thereby remaining within hearing distance of one another should we by chance encounter a wolf pack. It was not long before we heard a shot to the West of us, a sure sign that Bill had gotten lucky, no doubt bagging a buck. The Thlinget hunter has the reputation for never firing off a shot until he has his quarry directly in his sights.

Frank and I were proceeding in a cautious manner across some icy terrain, damnably aware of more swishy noises from our pants cuffs as they came in contact with the frozen brush. Luckily we came upon an area that was fairly clear, and since it seemed like a likeable spot to look for game, we plopped our butts down on some large mounds of mossy tundra, then commenced to blow our deer calls. Wouldn't you just know it? We succeeded in attracting the stool pigeon of the forest, a blabber-mouthed raven, that commenced raving from the top of an old snag nearby announcing to the world that, "Frankie and Johnnie are here." We merely conceded the point that this is part of the game and continued to blow our calls in an endeavor to attract some deer.

At this juncture in our philosophy on life, Frank gave me a gentle nudge to indicate he thought he heard something, while at the same time voiced his concern that everything had become unnaturally quiet. Where had ol' Mr. Raven gone? Then all in one motion he jumped to his feet to fire point blank straight ahead, while at the same time shouted, "John, wolves!" He missed, as the wolf he fired upon dove for cover behind a fallen log nearby.

We immediately became aware that there were several more wolves coming in on us in a "V" formation. "Don't move Frank," I hollered as I detected a wolf closing in on us from the left, but Frank was at this time concentrating on one other accosting him from his right side. By this time I could spot the wolf on his left getting uncomfortably close. I locked my sights on him. Then as he started around a small patch of brush, I aimed right at its leading edge. Just like the tomcat incident in Craig, the moment his nose appeared I moved the sights about an inch to the right and squeezed off the shot. The action that took place immediately following was the damndest thing I'd ever seen. The wolf stopped dead in it's tracks, sat back on it's haunches all in slow motion, then pointed it's muzzle skyward as if to howl. However, it made nary a sound as its mouth flew open and he just kind of folded down onto the ground.

We were extremely lucky that this broke up their attack, and although the wolf I had shot had not uttered a sound the rest of the pack immediately knew that one of their own was down. In spite of the fact that several shots had been fired and a member of the pack was down, the wolves began to circle round and round us, keeping up an incessant howling all the while. Both Frank and I fired several rounds apiece whenever we thought we saw the bushes move but still the pack continued circling while emitting their blood-curdling cries. You can't tell Frank and I that whoever invented the term blood-curdling, didn't know what they were talking about. I asked Frank later if his blood curdled, and he asked me the same thing. We both answered, YEP!

We stood our ground and fired a shot at any sign of movement until at long last the pack eventually withdrew, heading up a nearby arroyo still howling in the distance until silence once more took command of the situation, except for one small detail. Our hearts pounded like Voodoo drums in the entailing silence. With our rifles at the ready, we cautiously approached the log where the first wolf had dived for cover. To our utter amazement, he was gone. It was plain to see by the skid marks that he had flattened himself out to such an extent he had actually dragged himself along by his front legs with his back legs trailing behind. The exact tactics that a mouse employs when squeezing under a door. No wonder we had lost track of him during the excitement created during that wild melee.

After having regained a reasonable amount of composure I started over to where the dead wolf lay in order to claim my prize, but Frank insisted we get the heck outa there, pronto. "Hey, man," I reminded him. "That's fifty bucks laying out there." During the period before Alaska became a State, they were offering a bounty of $50.00 on wolves. I was intent on retrieving the nose and one forepaw which had to be turned in to the Fish and Game Dep't. in order to collect the bounty. After having accomplished this, I gutted the monster only to discover all he had in his stomach was a ball of grass. We assumed that this was how they survived lengthy periods of time without having anything to eat.

Oh, oh! We suddenly became aware of that unexplainable, eerie silence once more, so Frank suggested we climb a tree muchos quicko. I didn't need any prompting, believe me. No sooner were the words spoken, when we heard from the wolves again. They had somehow returned quietly as shadows, totally unobserved, then corralled us and set up the same pattern of circling and howling as before. Frank slammed his rifle into my hands then vaulted up a tree commanding me to, "Quick, hand me my rifle and I'll cover for you." "Hurry John, hand me your rifle, don't worry, I'm covering for you."

Yikes, there's likely to be thirty savage wolves in this gang who appear to be desperate and famished, beside the fact they have the scent of blood from the animal I had just recently gutted. This made the wolves akin to a school of sharks all riled up and eager to strike. So what's to worry? Hah! Frankie's asking me to strip myself bare of the only means of protection I have, by letting go of my rifle. Still, hadn't we been informed innumerous times previous to this incident that wolves will not attack humans? So now I'm wondering, "Why in blazes hadn't these stupid wolves been informed of this?"

It demanded every ounce of intestinal fortitude I could muster in order for me to release my rifle before skyrocketing upward to where Frank stood, braced to fire, should the need arise. On that slow, draggy flight upward, I swear I could almost feel those horrible fangs sinking into that vulnerable part of my anatomy, before I finally got treed!

In the meantime both Bill and Leo had been alerted to the fact that Frank and I could be in real trouble as they rushed to assist us by firing into the outer ring of the pack. It was all over in a matter of minutes as the wolves took off for the same arroyo, but this time for good. Bill was of the opinion that the wolves weren't after Frank and I the second time they returned. He felt they were intent on driving us away from the kill so they might devour it. "Devour," that word sure stuck in our minds. Well in spite of it all we surely had an interesting tale to tell, and we still feel that we were very lucky that we didn't end up being wolf-fodder.

During a later discussion it was clarified that the circling and howling tactics performed by the pack was merely a ploy to keep their quarry corralled. Therefore, the several wolves that entered the enclosure would be assured the object of their affection would not be offered the opportunity to escape.

LOVE IN BLOOM

Folks, in the event that an incident involving a sexual encounter might offend you, simply do not read this chapter, okay?

There were three happy-go-lucky old winos in town, all bearing the name, Willie, a trio who were cheerful, friendly, and full of life. In fact I enjoyed a solid and friendly relationship with all three, kidding them whenever I spotted them together. It happened that this morning I accosted them just as they were tying up at our float after a trip into Craig in their little putt, putt. As usual after a trip to Craig they arrived well supplied with jugs of wine as they headed for the jungle, a name bestowed upon their residence which was located far back in a wooded area just outside the cannery property.

I want you to recall my reason for living in Klawock was to preside as caretaker for Libby's interests while the transformation to rebuild their cannery was in progress. We had reached that stage, the cannery had been operable, and it was now my duty to ship the salmon pack, numbering 47,000 cases, to Seattle via the Alaska Steamship Co.

I chanced to be standing on the dock at the time when the three Willies came clambering up the ramp as quietly as a high school cheerleading section. Nevertheless, I was elated in seeing them since this was part of my longshoring crew. In spotting me on the dock, they all three, amidst resounding guffaws and a volley of pats on my back, laughed aloud as I chided them, "You guys give me the Willies." In retaliation I was offered a "Slug outa the jug." which sent them into a panic because of the fact that they had made a pun.

Willie Jackson had a voice on him that carried like the horn on an eighteen wheeler, while Willie Skinnah spoke so softly he couldn't be heard. Willie Chuck just kinda grinned all the time leading me to think he had consumed more than his share of el' juggo.

In order that I not rub them the wrong way, I offered. "Sorry guys, I can't drink anything right now, I got a ship coming in for the salmon pack in a couple of days, so I have to get busy and recount the pack, wasaw? You guys gotta promise you gonna come to longshore for me, okay?" "Okay! We gonna be there."

No offense was taken since this was an acceptable excuse. They each hooked their fingers into a jug of wine and headed for their dear little home in the West, somewhat resembling a trio of beautiful Christmas trees displaying colorful shiny ornaments dangling from their limbs. I was extremely thankful that I had extracted from them a promise that they would show up for longshoring since Halibut season was on and manpower within the village was at a premium.

Barely an hour had transpired since my encounter with the three Willies, when who happened by? None other than vivacious Katie Kooch, five foot two, eyes of blue, weight two hundred and twenty two. To claim she was promiscuous was to put it mildly. Somehow she had gotten the scent of wine, or more than likely it was pre-arranged. Nevertheless, she was definitely headed for the jungle.

This happened to be on a Monday. I had already dismissed the matter from my mind by the time Wednesday had rolled around, when I received a radio message that the ship was approaching Klawock to load out the salmon pack for delivery to Seattle. This prompted me to get busy and round up a longshore crew, which I attempted by soliciting throughout the village for manpower.

Following this I set out to round up the three Willles. When I arrived at their shack I thought there must be one gigantis biggo argument going on, judging from the amount of noise reverberating from inside the walls. I rapped loudly on the door several times before Willie Skinnah finally opened it to welcome me in. What a shock it was for me to discover the wine party still in full swing from last Monday. Everyone was conversing at the top of their lungs, the house was a disaster with dirty pots, pans and dishes, piled high all over the place, even in the corner of the room that sufficed as the bedroom. Most of the activity and noise was centered in this portion of the house.

Being enacted right before my eyes was something I'd heard about but had never actually encountered. Willie Chuck was just in the act of dismounting from Katie while Willie Jackson was maneuvering into position to take his place. Then at the same time, Willie Skinnah was endeavoring to make himself heard in announcing that I had arrived, but all in the same breath, was also reprimanding Willie Jackson to get off and give Johnnie a turn. All this is happening at split second intervals even while Katie has given Willie a solid rap alongside the head. Willie is bellering in his finest fog horn salvo, "Hey! how come you done that?" Then it suddenly dawns on Willie why Katie is distraught as he reaches down to detach an empty jug from Katie's limp grasp. Immediately upon sensing a full jug on her finger, Katie gives the signal, "Okay, go ahet." But instead, Willie obligingly forfeited his turn, offering that I was to take his place.

All the while I'm protesting vehemently that I can't possibly stay since I have a ship arriving shortly. I have to be prepared to load out the salmon. I just came by to tell you guys I'll need you in the morning for longshoring. Meanwhile, Katie, bless her lovely face, is beckoning me with open arms, the starlight gleaming in her azure blue eyes. (I read that somewhere. It seems so fitting for the occasion). Actually, Katie has extremely dark eyes, besides looking as huge as a beaver dam with her legs spread invitingly, displaying an incredible sight. Wow, was I ever relieved to get out of there post haste, and back into the world of reality once again.

BEARLY MISSED

Ya know what boat's a-comin'. Ya know daylight's just breaking. You're wishin' it wasn't this damn early, and you've guessed it's another huntin' trip.

Okay, now that the colorful introduction for this chapter has been dealt with, betcha can't guess, "what hoppened?" It aint like something that might occur in downtown Kalamazoo, and that's what makes it so unique. Animals in Alaska are rough and tough. They ask no quarter and give no quarter, that is why every time you enter their domain anything can happen and oft times does!

You can rest assured that if you were out in this wilderness alone without the guidance of the Indian, you most assuredly would be dead by now. So I offer this incident as another tidbit of knowledge toward your understanding of, "An Alaska that Used To Was."

I have a different partner on this sojourn into adventure since Bill had other things to do. His name is Aaron Isaacs, Sr. "Good morning Johnnie, sure hope this rain keeps up," his first words for the day. "You do?" "How come?" "So it don't come down!" A good sound slap on the back followed by a booming fit of laughter. That's my partner for today.

As usual we've picked our spot, a small bull pine sitting atop a knoll affording us a splendid view in all directions. The broad muskeg spread out before us is littered with small bull pines and small bunches of brush, ideal cover for deer. We're sitting back to back against the tree, a common practice for ones own safety as well as your partners. Aaron has commenced calling, with his deer call hanging from his neck and his rifle lying dormant across his lap. After quite a lapse in time with no takers, Aaron gives me that slight nudge in the ribs indicating he's heard or spotted something.

Our only warning came when we heard a loud WOOF as a large, black bear burst out of the brush taking a swipe at Aaron following his initial charge. Poof, just like magic the whole sleeve of his mackinaw disappeared from the shoulder to the wrist. At the same time Aaron instinctively hauled back on the trigger of his rifle which fortunately was pointed in the right direction, pounding the bear with a 30-30 slug directly in his undercarriage. This forced the bear to go tumbling backwards off the knoll while at the same time Aaron and I were laying little puffs of smoke in our wake as we nonchalantly rocketed elsewhere. After our initial mad gallop out of there plus detecting no sounds of pursuit, we mustered enough courage to cautiously sneak back for a look-see. There lay Mr. Bruin at the bottom of the incline. Being aware that to knock off a large bear with only one shot was very unlikey, we approached tipsy toesy with our rifles at the ready, but it proved out to be that the bear was permanently, dead. That's the best kind of dead out here in the wilds. After checking the bear over we decided the bullet had pierced his heart and lungs since Aaron had fired point blank into the bear's underbelly.

Apparently the bear had just come out of hibernation cause the meat was almost similar in consistency to beef. However, if he'd been out of hibernation for any length of time it would have been another story. The meat then, would have been equivalent to sitting down to a dinner of Mexican Fighting cocks.

Sure, everyone tells us that wolves won't attack humans. I suppose we'll be told bears don't attack humans, also. Both Aaron and I appreciate this fact, but we still have our doubts as to whether this little fable, verily rings true.

THE LEGEND OF KUSH DA KAH

Kush Da Kah, "Land Otter, man." This legend should have remained a legend, but it did not. Rather than that, it possessed our little village and became a shocking reality.

The Thlinget Indians hold to a belief that whenever one of their family members should be drowned and the body not recovered, it becomes a certainty, Kush Da Kah got'em. This is the case with one George McNeil.

The Thlingets firmly believe the land otter rescues the drowning person before he actually drowns, then takes him to their lair where he shall remain for a period of three years to be raised as one of their own. The capture, supposedly is accomplished through the otters casting a spell upon that person much the same as hypnotism. After the expiration of this three year term, if the victim can by any means break the hypnotic spell he would then be offered new life and the opportunity to return to his original status as a human. Otherwise, he shall remain as a land otter forever.

This is what the natives called coming back.

Several days away from the three-year period when one George McNeil was presumed drowned and the body never recovered, word got out that George was coming back. The whole affair started when Edna McNeil, George's wife insisted that she had had visions of George making an effort to come back. As relentlessly as a lava flow the rumor spread throughout the village. It wasn't long before the whole town became, hysterically motivated, as friends and relatives both near and far were notified of this unbelievable possibility.

Correction, please! Rather than an air of excitement, it was fear that became the dominant factor throughout the village, immediately following the announcement that Kush Da Kah was to pay a visit to the town, most inhabitants of the village were too frightened to venture forth at night. Even more so, after the Shaman warned everyone they were to expect George's body to be completely covered over with long matted hair.

Incidentally, the cannery was all set up with a short wave, radio communication service, with A-L-E, Ketchikan, so consequently I was in charge of all long distance phone calls within and outside of Klawock. At this period in time the phone was one of those instruments where you had to compress the trigger in order to transmit or receive. Therefore it became necessary that you say, "Over," as you release the button to receive conversation from the other party.

During the ensuing crisis, it was generally the older women of the tribe who were placing calls stateside. This proved to be kind of entertaining for me in a way, because they had difficulty in compressing or depressing the button at the right times. So it went like this. Hello - - - Hello? Push the button Elsie. Hello, Rudy, can you hear me? Push the button and say over! "Oafer" "Release the button, Elsie, he can't answer you. "Okay!" "Yeah maw, I hear you, is it true Uncle George is coming back? Over." "Yes, can you come home?" "Push the button Elsie." "Oh! Can you come home? Oafer." "Release the button, Elsie," etc, etc, etc. I'm sure you get the picture.

In the meantime things are getting proportionately worse. Our Shaman, Spencer Williams, Sr. had informed everyone, in addition to being hairy George should appear to be very wild with deep piercing eyes, and also would be crawling on all fours like a crazed animal, painting a terribly intimidating picture in their minds to say the least.

Mary Dick was an old Thlinget lady who resided in Klawock, but just outside the city limits. In other words, she lived on the other side of the tracks, so to speak. She was as usual, very unkempt, snaggle toothed, wrinkled, and stooped. One who much preferred a shot of wine to combing her hair, but nevertheless commanded a token greeting from those who chanced to pass her on the road. Of all things, darned if Mary hadn't taken to wandering about the streets the same night when George was expected to come back. Unfortunately, she was accosted by the night guard, the men in the village who were all tensed and spooked to begin with. In spotting Mary out on this particularly ominous night, it led them to believe she was some kind of evil spirit, a bad omen. What other reason could there possibly be that this old hag, who in their eyes resembled a witch, was caught wandering around in the darkness at this particular time?

"Of course I was there, I'm trying to learn, right?" Only I was not a believer, so it really shocked me to witness cool guys, well educated guys, guys that I could easily call friends, suddenly revert back to spookyism, even to the point where they had detained poor old Mary. How fortunate for this poor old lady, our mayor, Ed Peratrovich, happened along at the same time the night guard had way-layed her. She could easily have suffered bodily harm. Ed interceded in her behalf as an interpreter for her slurred Thlinget explanation. It turned out Mary had been drinking and was unaware of the danger involved should she venture out this night of all nights. Mary had simply run out of snoose so was heading for her neighbors place to get some.

This incident proves beyond a doubt that the use of snoose could be harmful to ones health.

For several days preceding George's arrival, plans were being made to capture the Kush Da Kah. Those who had volunteered to assist the Shaman in bringing George back could be observed packing knives and weapons upon their persons. Even this was contrary to their normal conduct.

Things are really booming along now as the prospect of capturing George has escalated into unGodly proportions. Spencer Williams, our Shaman has instructed his assistants that it will be necessary to detain George long enough so that he could accomplish a laying-on of hands in order to break the hypnotic spell Kush Da Kah is under. I truly believe the Shaman is feeling center stage in this progressive drama, as various plans are brought to the fore in order to achieve the capture.

In fact a group of men, led by another self appointed medicine man, Robert Snook, had devised a plan where they commenced fastening a whole bunch of fishhooks, into a large section of netting. The next phase of their plan was to then spread the netting all over the bushes covering an area surrounding George's house, because logic dictated that this is where George was bound to turn up. Thus, when he got caught in the webbing and became entangled with the hooks, the crew of men could immediately jump on him to wrestle him down to the ground. Good thinking you guys, I think?

Spencer and Robert Snook, both self appointed Sahmen, joined forces in a plan so astonishingly simple, it had to work. Wait until you hear it. In fact, I'm kinda worried you will interpret the word simple, as simple, but it is your choice.

I watched in amazement, as they began stringing ropes from the trees and bushes surrounding Kush Da Kah's house. The Shamen requested that they refer to George as Kush Da Kah from here on in, which I'm certain was primarily a ploy for the medicine man to create a more dramatic approach to all that is taking place at this time.

The ropes were then impregnated with shards of bone taken from the leg bones of a dog. Spencer and I had good repoire with one another, no doubt stemming from the time I had saved his boat from sinking at an earlier point in time.

Therefore, he had no qualms about taking me into his confidence as he came forward and offered me an educational explanation for his actions.

"Johnnie," he spoke very gutteral and in broken english since he habitually spoke in the Thlinget dialect when conversing during his daily activities. "Johnnie, he continued, "I putting dis dog bones through the rope cause dis the ones make the sharp points when you pound them on the rocks." "I gonna hold my hand like dis, see, they don't touched the bones when I sliding them up and down the rope." He demonstrated by actually cupping his hands around the sharp shards of bone as he traveled back and forth the length of the rope, meanwhile, chanting in a weird sounding, high-pitched sing song manner. If you can think of a better way to describe it, feel free my friends.

The hackles on the back of my neck stood at attention with no prompting on my part whatsoever, as I became cognizant of the fact, here I am, involved in witnessing a form of Voodooism that most assuredly did not originate in Africa. Man I could hardly believe what I was seeing.

Right now I have to take time out to feel sorry for those in the village indirectly involved, in all the shenanigans that have been going on for several days over Kush Da Kah's upcoming visit. It's sad to observe the looks on their faces reflecting the amount of fear and anxiety they are suffering over this bit of "Hell on Earth."

To continue, Spencer returned from his demonstration to further advise me, "Kush Da Kah, with his sharp eyes is looking to me from the bushes, so he seen me and heard my message to copy what I just done.

Now! He copied me and gotten stucked by the bone. Aha! When he's kneeled down cause he got stuckeded and it hurt, now we can jump on him to break the spell, Wasaw?" (undertand) I didn't dare say it, but surely thought it. Isn't this a little far-fetched, then I learned a bit later it was the chant they considered to be the primary factor in encouraging Kush Da Kah to engage himself in the rope trick. Unfortunately, I was unable to cover all phases of get Kush Da Kah, and undoubtedly there were others, so eventually everything was in readiness and we had but one recourse, "WAIT!"

Have you not heard of a town waiting out a hurricane? Well there's quite a similarity here. A common fear presided over the entire town. It's as though a violent twister was heading their way. Will it hit or not? Let's pray it might possibly go around us, etc. All, have one frighteningly tense situation to deal with.

From my point of view the whole thing amounted to a combination of mass hypnosis, coupled with mass hysteria, affecting everyone within its scope. Unbelievably, I'm witnessing college-educated persons, as well as the uneducated, reverting to something bordering on Witchcraft at this late period in time. It threw me for a loop. A whole village trembling for fear of the unknown. "How?" I wondered, "Could this be?"

This is it! The big night has caught up to us but the main feature turned out to be a complete flop. The main star, Kush Da Kah failed to appear for his premier performance.

However, there still remains a shadow of doubt since there were those who ascertained, "Oh yes, I know I heard something." Or, "I'm sure I saw something moving in the bushes, from my window." Etc. Incredibly, everything settled down to normal in less than three days, as Kush Da Kah reverted into being a legend, as before, Nevertheless, I am rather reluctant to judge or pass judgement, for aren't we equally guilty of the same conduct?

Come on now, you doubters. Don't tell me you haven't heard of children being threatened with, "Eat your mush or the boogie man's gonna getchoo!" "The tooth fairy is going to leave you some money if you'll just sit still long enough for me to me yank that stupid tooth outa your face, darling." "Santa Claus is coming to town so you better be nice cause he knows if you've got them sly lil' peepers open, then he won't come down the chimney. Course he won't when he's got one helluva big belly, and the chimney is no larger than six or eight inches in diameter. There are times when I wonder just how bright we are, ourselves.

There's always the one about the Indian questioning our practice of putting flowers on the gravesites. He asks, "what they gonna do, sit up and smell'um?"

Enough is enough. So much for any further discussion governing legends and human nature. I promised an Alaska you never dreamed existed. Okay, this is simply another slice of it.

THE GEESE HUNTER

Today you will find the three of us, Frank, Leo and myself, churning up the water in a fourteen-foot skiff. We're moving along at a pretty good clip, due to the efforts from a 35 horsepower Evinrude outboard motor. The sky is quite the opposite of the norm today since it is blue for a change. We've timed it just right and the water is now at slack tide. We've learned that the geese have shown up in Shinaku, so look out you plump breasted members of the goose family. Here we come.

Shinaku at this moment is a huge saltwater lake, but within twelve hours time shall become nothing more than an empty saucer. During that period when the tide is coming in, salt water is fed into Shinaku through a small opening called a Chuck. As the tide rises, water jets through the Chuck, increasing the size and the depth of the lake, considerably. Then again as the tide recedes, it has just the opposite affect. The water jets back out again, causing the lake to become nothing more than a mud flat.

Therefore, for this reason we must time our entry into Shinaku just before high, slack-tide. This is when the water gushing into the lake has reached its highest level and has slowed to a crawl before becoming completely calm. Soon thereafter, a reverse motion will begin which in a very short time will turn into a raging torrent of water. If one dared challenge it they would find it quite capable of capsizing the skiff, besides pulling its occupants under and out of sight due to the terrific undertow created by this immense volume of water spewing through the small opening, named skookumchuck.

Our timing was just right for entering the Chuck. The water was nearly at a standstill which granted us a little more than three hours of fowl hunting before we would be forced to get back out. Since this was my very first lesson in the art of hunting geese, and also since I owned no shotgun of my own, Papa George, the person responsible for having me adopted into the tribe, had volunteered his shotgun for me to use. Leo and Frank made sure I was positioned in the bow of the boat so that I would be assured of a clear shot in the event we got within range of a goose. (I'm sure they extended me that courtesy because they were quite possibly thinking about a shot that might go clear through their head.)

After a short period of cruising the lake, Frank spotted a goose flying directly toward us and immediately offered me the opportunity to get the first shot in, hollering, "Get ready Johnnie, here comes one." Good grief, the bird looked no larger than a hummingbird it was flying so high, but fortunately its flight pattern indicated that it would be flying directly over us. As Leo slowed the skiff to a crawl, I upped the shotgun, yanked back on the trigger, then "BLOOIE," an unseen force smashed into my shoulder, literally jerking my head off it's hinges. I was knocked backward on my butt into the bottom of the skiff while the shotgun came clattering around me in several pieces.

At the same time Leo and Frank were ecstatic. They both had tears running down their faces due to their uncontrollable laughter, and they were yelling, "Ya got'im," "I'll be damned, ya got'im." Wow what a shot! They then rushed over to retrieve the bird while at the same time kept egging me on, "Grab him quick John, or he'll get away, wring it's neck, hurry, ring it's neck."

Man alive what a strange and repulsive feeling when I wrapped my fingers around its throat in an attempt to wring the damn bird's neck. What in blazes, it was as slippery as two banana peels wrapped around a piece of plastic pipe. Both Leo and Frank were in stitches, the tears literally pouring down their cheeks, while here am I, suffering total confusion, wondering how in the heck could anyone even begin to wring the neck of this slithering snake like object. Frank flashed past me, grasped the goose by the head, and simply spun it in one deft motion, thus breaking its neck. He then hauled it aboard in one swift move, tossing it at my feet. Both he and Leo commenced to shower me with praise for the great shot I had made. They excitedly, continued to slap me on the back just to emphasize how lucky I was to nail such a dandy geese, especially on my first time out.

It struck me as kinda strange that their laughter and tears didn't diminish as rapidly as I thought they should, but I attributed their carrying on as perhaps a pat on the back for themselves for teaching me so well.

Leo yanked the motor back into service once more, as it was time to get the H--- outa there pronto if we were going to make our escape through the Chuck.

On the way back to Klawock the boys repeatedly relived the incident, elaborating on what a difficult shot I had made. "Man oh man but that geese was high, wow what a shot," then again commenting as to how lucky I was to get a geese on my first time out. I wasn't about to embarrass them by correcting their use of English when calling a goose a geese.

We arrived back in Klawock without further incident, but as we progressed through town I was encouraged to present my trophy to those inquiring if I had been successful, so I oft times held up my prize to show them my goose. For some unknown reason my eager response to present my prize caused an unusual amount of laughter. In addition to that it appeared to create an unusual amount of red faces also, every time I offered to show someone my goose.

(I'm getting suspicious that something's amiss.)
(You, too?)

After reaching the sanctity of Papa George's house in order to return the shotgun, I immediately apologized that his gun had fallen apart. He brushed that aside with a grin, informing me that this always happened, he had simply forgotten to forewarn me of that. Aha! I'm beginning to think that maybe I was set up for this little drama. "Damn Indians, they're not supposed to have this great a sense of humor." After a courteous pause, (the Indian way) my big Thlinget daddy discreetly inquired if I had been successful in shooting a geese, so I proudly held up my goose for him, and he too, like all the others turned grin-faced, and red. Papa George now turned serious. In a whisper, he secretly cautioned me. "Johnnie, don't say that one you said, say geese, the one you said are a woman's thing." He pointed to his lap, while needless to say, I in turn, blossomed out with a face redder than any of those I had witnessed that day.

Much to my chagrin, I'll just have to suffer through telling you the rest of the story. (Good sport, aye?))

Seemingly, as though taking me into his strictest confidence, Papa George whispered, "Johnnie, that one you have there, he's not a geese. You shooted a loon. Maybe the boys are funnin you!" Egads, I immediately did a flashback, recalling the time when I first arrived on the airplane float in Klawock. At that time I tried to impress all those kids as to how we hunted ducks where I came from by hitting golf balls at them. I'm now certain in my mind this is all in retaliation for the funnin I had done them, but that seemed like eons ago.

"Hell's fire, can't they take a joke?"

Nevertheless, I've condescended to name this chapter, 'THE GEESE HUNTER!"

I'm certain ya all understand why.

EXOTIC FOOD

During our travels through this land of plenty, we've definitely established one thing for sure. You most certainly don't have to go to the fish market for fish. All one has to do is go out into their front yard and catch'em.

Now I wonder? "How come so many people catche'm, then ruin'em?"

It seems the average person attempts to cook fish in large chunks like, yum, yum, look at that nice big filet of red snapper sizzling in the pan. More than likely it'll turn out half cooked in some places but too darned dry all around the perimeter. The trick in cooking all varieties of fish is to cut the pieces into smaller elongated strips. Following this, a light coating of miracle whip is applied in place of flour or cornmeal, which is the common practice. At this mid-point in preparing your fish for dinner, by all means fry the fish in a very hot skillet and quickly, while at the same time make sure you have an ample amount of crisco or cooking oil in the pan. The meat will turn white in a very short time, a sign that it is done and ready to serve. The end result will astound you as the fish shall be nice and evenly browned, cooked all the way through, but still retain all it's natural moisture, making it scrumptious and mouthwateringly delicious.

Have you by chance heard of Yane, the Thlinget name for the Sea Cucumber? It goes by the name of Trepang in the commercial markets, where it is most likely to be available in some of the fancier restaurants throughout the Eastern states. The sea cucumber is equally as luscious as it is ugly. It actually resembles an oversized snail, covered with spiny but soft, tapered and conical, curved, horny looking node-like apertures, protruding from all angles of it's body as it crawls around the kelp infested ocean floor. Bearing a strong resemblance to the common snail you see in your flower garden, this ugly "thing" keeps on eating, and eating, and eating incessantly. Irregardless of how it looks, this hideous looking slug when fried in butter will reward you with a surprisingly pleasant taste, equally as appealing as the succulent flavor of a razor clam.

However, preparing the Yane for frying is somewhat of a challenge as the skin is as tough as shoe leather, but once you separate that wonderful strip of razor clam meat from the skin, therein lies a gourmet treat. It is first necessary that you cut off the feeding end of the yane to insert your knife in the opened end then slit the thing all the way through to the other end, laying it open like a book. A pair of pliers is an absolute necessity at this point, as you must now get a good solid grip on the tough hide while sliding your knife blade between the skin and the meat. Okay, now pull hard with the pliers, and slide hard with the knife blade. "VOILA" You have extracted a strip of white meat equivalent to a razor clam, all ready to pop into a good hot skillet for no more than ¾ of a minute, thereby granting yourself a treat well worth the effort.

(Me too,) I'm also wondering how they found out this "thing" was good to eat in the first place.

And now here's the big one for exotic food.

Fish egg season always occurs with the arrival of springtime here in S.E. Alaska. It heralds the arrival of millions and trillions, even thousands of herring, all intent on but one thing. Reproduction!

Their arrival also heralds an air of festive activity throughout the area as old and young alike prepare to harvest herring roe. The herring converge en masse, upon an Island located in the main channel between Craig and Klawock, actually named Fish Egg Island. When the time has arrived for the herring to spawn, the females arrive in such huge numbers they actually turn the water black as far as the eye can see, there are that many fish in the inlet. They deposit their eggs on anything the eggs can adhere to. They seek out rocks, kelp, and especially a fallen branch lying in the water. These herring are pretty good sized, running like 12 and 13 inches in length. They definitely resemble a large smelt and surprisingly the meat is also similar in flavor and consistency to the smelt, the only difference being that the herrings bone is a lot tougher. However, this actually offers one an advantage because this toughness makes it much easier to remove the bone from the herring in comparison to the other. Needless to say, the herring are delicious although the Indians actually prefer the roe.

The natives gather the roe in the following manner, while at the same time initiate a fish egg festival in honor of the occasion. After gathering strands and strands of spruce boughs they are tied together, several in a cluster then again the cluster of branches is made fast to a good-sized rock where they are submerged directly in the path of the spawning herring.

After the submerged branches have gone through a tide change they are then retrieved, heavily coated with nearly five to six inches of solid roe. Believe me they weigh a darn good grunt when you lift them from the water. The caviar is taken and prepared for eating simply by submerging the eggs, branches and all into a large kettle of boiling sea water. Within a matter of from 20 to 30 seconds the eggs, which are somewhat yellowish in color, will turn chalk white. This is an indication that they are sufficiently done at which time you plop a big lump of butter into the top of the pot before you extract the eggs so that as you draw the eggs from the pot they are liberally coated with butter.

This is the moment when you eagerly rip off big globs of Alaska caviar, completely oblivious to the fact that the butter is running off your chin clear down to your elbows. As though mesmerized, you stand entranced pigging out on one of the most delectable and enjoyable treats of a lifetime.

Huh! If there's a possibility you don't engage in this sort of thing, then just forget it and skip this chapter if that's the way you wanna be, okay?

Maybe this would tickle your palate more than the luscious caviar I just described.

Did you know that the Dungeness crab abounds here in S.E. Alaska. They may be found in nearly every grassy-bottomed estuary throughout the area surrounding Klawock. To my way of thinking they are far superior to the Alaska King Crab that is presently permeating the market. The dungeness crab is easily identified by a pair of huge pincers in front, that should they get hold of your finger, are powerful enough to make you lose the nail. They are nice large crab, measuring from nine to ten inches across the back, and posses a flavor that to my notion surpasses that of both the King crab and Snow crab, which are harvested in the Kodiak area. In order to utilize all portions of the crab, especially the legs, I devised a system for fattening the skinny buzzards much the same way as the good ol' farmer back in Iowa fattens hogs, and here's how I did it.

First of all I constructed a wire basket made from chicken wire, large enough to retain a dozen or more live crab. I then fastened it alongside the float while making certain it was sticking up out of the water at least a foot. Should any of the crab manage to climb to the top of the basket they would be unable to escape since there would be no water to afford them the buoyancy they would need to go over the top. At this point a jellyfish scoop was brought into play. There were at certain tides, a multitude of little white jellyfish being transported along with the current. These I brailed into the basket containing the live crab, and they immediately went yummy, yum, yum, literally gourmandizing themselves to death over this unexpected feast. The crab actually became so fat and full-bodied from the jelly fish banquet, that after they were cooked and ready to be eaten there was no such thing as having to pick the meat from the leg sections as before. Instead, all one had to do was bang them with the heel of the hand and they would actually pop open like an eggshell with the meat fairly falling into your hands.

We have finally arrived at the end of my desertation concerning a number of, the out of the ordinary foods we enjoy up here in the North Country. Bear with me just a bit longer folks, cause I feel it necessary to expostulate on one more subject.

"The art of cooking and enjoying Octopii. Incidentally, the lady of the house should be the one to act upon the following instructions. "Should your hubby by any fluke of ill fortune arrive home toting of all things a nice piece of Octopus meat, you should without the slightest hesitation beg borrow or steal a sixteen pound sledge hammer. You must then sneak out into hubbies work shop where you shall hope and pray he has an anvil available. Place the meat upon the anvil. Inhale deeply! Now muster up three of your very best slams with the sledge hammer which will without a doubt assure you the damn thing is dead, anyway.

I would now recommend that you obtain a couple pieces of at least ¾" plywood, (it has to be strong, you know) then place the octopus meat between them out in your driveway. You should now run the car back and forth over it about twelve times or so. This serves to make one helluva mess out of the damn thing, granting you a reasonable excuse for tossing it into the garbage. Now sneak back into the house and commence to kitchie koo honey, which by all means should definitely distract him to the point where he aint gonna be thinkin bout no lousy chunk of octopus.

That's the best I can do ya on octopus, dearie, except if one had enough of them and had a mould handy, you could become filthy rich by developing an automobile tire that would damn sure last forever.

A NEAR TRAGEDY!

Fate can be either cruel, or kind. In this instance she chose to be kind, to spare us from the forthcoming tragedy of a small child losing his life to a bout with pneumonia.

It had to do with an afternoon while I was cruising the cannery premises to make sure that everything was in order, when I spotted my friend and buddy Frank Woods, who's home was adjacent to the cannery premises. He appeared to be so unnaturally solemn and downcast that I was forced to confront him to ask if something was wrong. His reply really jolted me as he informed me in a barely audible whisper, obviously making an effort to choke back the tears, "My son's dying, Johnnie, do you want to see him before he is dead?"

Of course I did, so I hurried over to the house with Frank to discover the Indian mourners already sitting in a circle around, "Little John", Frank and Joanna Woods two year old son who, incidentally, had been named after me. He was barely breathing and his lips were already turning blue. To this day I have no idea what prompted me to react as though I knew what I was doing, but I ran outside to commandeer a couple of stout male relatives to Little John, ordering that they should come with me, immediately. (Chuuk) "Hurry you guys come with me," I commanded as I rushed back down to the cannery. Inside the blacksmith shop I had a big old iron-wheeled hand truck upon which was mounted two large cylinders. One was an acetylene tank weighing upwards of 100 lbs. while the other cylinder contained oxygen for welding and it too was plenty heavy, weighing close to 85 lbs.

"Hurry you guys, bring the tanks to the house." No questions were asked, they did my bidding without any hesitation on their part. I knew for sure I couldn't have hauled this hormongous monstrosity over that gravelly road by any means, but those two husky Indian lads did it. Thank you, Lenny Armour, and Rudy Smith.

Upon reaching the house I strung the welding hoses right into the front room where they had the baby. I then turned on the oxygen bottle, inserted the tip of the cutting torch gently but barely inside the baby's nostril and so let Little John partake of a gentle flow of oxygen. Within a very few minutes that seemed like hours, a miracle took place. I noticed the blue around Little Johns lips begin to take on a rosy hue, then miraculously, the baby commenced breathing really well on his own. Both Frank and Joanna broke into tears as they held their baby close in their arms, and I had to choke back some tears of my own.

Shortly thereafter, the mourners picked up and left with only one, offering a comment of any kind. It was the eldest of the group who said, "They named dis one good." "You the one kept him alive, Konas Chees!" (Thank You) Then she left. It was such a great ending for all. Fortunately for me, the boys returned my welding cart. Frankie and Joanna held their baby close in their arms, and I rode off into the sunset on my mighty steed. Okay, so I didn't have a horse. At a time like this do ya have to be so picky? Could be the welding cart was my mighty steed.

A HAPPY FOURTH OF JULY 2-U-2

I might again remind you, when the salmon run is on it is the machinists obligation to see that the canning machinery remains operable and that the salmon being delivered into the cannery, no matter what the amount, is promptly processed. Sure they make good money but there are times when they are forced to pay a fair price for the privilege. For example;

After a particularly long and drawn out canning period when the salmon kept coming and coming and coming, our Superintendent found it necessary that he put his machinist crew through an ungodly stretch of long hours. Following this, the Old Man, the Head Honcho, out of the goodness of his heart, announced, "We're gonna shut'er down boys, everyone gets the Fourth of July off." We found out the fish and Game Commission had closed the fishing over the holidays so decided the bit about, out of the goodness of his heart was nothing more than gas from his lower abdomen. We felt sure he was more concerned that there wouldn't be enough hearses available for all, should he continue with this 22-24 hr work program.

The entire machinist gang had reached a point where they smelled a lot, like older than old garbage. Stop to consider the fact that none of them had had the opportunity to shower or wash clothes for more than a week. Do not be misled that jungle rot originates from wading the swamps in Nam. Woosh! Some of the machinist's feet could easily compete with a chunk of spoiled fish. In making a comparison with the old socks strewn about the bunk house, and some dead fish laying on the beach, I'm afraid it would be my choice to award the bunk house socks the edge for being the most offensive and odorous of the two.

On the third of July at 5:00 O'clock in the afternoon, we were granted our leave. What a fiasco that turned out to be. The cannery had furnished us with but two washing machines that were supposed to convert something like thirty two ugh-ly coveralls into sweet smelling hunks of clothing in one simple operation. In order that we might solve the dilemma as to who's going to sleep and who's going to get the washing machine, we decided that we would draw straws. It turned out that I was one of the lucky ones. I drew sleep. One of the guys offered to toss in a pair of my coveralls at the same time he did several others, so I blasted off to the bunk house to grab some of that wonderful stuff called slumber.

Baloney! Didja ever try to go to sleep after you've been accustomed to not getting any, all during the previous week. Instead, I found myself lying there staring at the ceiling with my eyes wide open, while visions of sugar plumbs danced through my wee little head. Oops, scuse preaze, that's Xmas stuff! Just the same it was a weird feeling, so I got back on my feet to wander zombie-like into the recreation room, only to find the rest of the gang suffering from the same phobia. An old timer, the most intelligent member of our gang (?), advised us the only way any of us would get any sleep was to partake of a relaxing agent by the name of Jack Daniels, or his cousin Mr. Seagrams.

Klawock was what they called a dry town because of it's being and Indian village. Therefore, it became necessary that someone of our group must make a trip to Craig since it was well stocked with relaxing agents. Very good guess there, friends. Yes, it was I who got the assignment for the trip to Craig, simply because I knew the area and also knew all the Cabbies in town. All the Cabbies in town was Fred Anniskette. Both he and his cab were 73 yrs old, I'm sure. The road to Craig was more like a cow path, hugging rocky cliffs in addition to bordering the ocean all the way to our destination. The road had been scratched out of rocks and brush by the U.S. Forest Service, for what purpose I am at a loss to understand.

In the meantime I had commandeered Fred, who guaranteed that we would be in Craig within a half-hours time. Fred then proceeded to transform himself from being an elderly Thlinget Indian into becoming a classy looking New York cabbie, by donning a leather cap with a black visor, and ahem!, was now all set to transport us into town. Two others of our gang had decided to accompany us as they were interested in seeing what Craig looked like. Fred was all set to go, provided that he had $16.00 planted firmly in his hand before he would start the motor. After fulfilling his request we embarked upon our errand of mercy. "It must cost you to $20.00 for I'm bringing you back," we were advised. "Johnnie, I driving to Craig makes me tired, so I charging some more to comin back cause I gotten more tired." Made cents to me, I think?

Previous to this time I had lived in Craig for a good while, so naturally was well acquainted with most of the townsfolk, but my duties in Klawock had prevented me from visiting Craig that often so the Caig-ites were more or less laying for me. Upon entering the bar and purchasing our relaxers, it seemed to me that all I heard from this point on, was "Hey, buy Johnnie a drink, hey buy Johnnie a drink. Man oh man, they were coming at me one after another. Everyone it seemed, was glad to see me. By this time I had spent quite a bit of time yacking with my old friends while partaking of a few cocktails myself. I came to realize there were at least ten more drinks on the table that were mine. I decided it was imperative that I vacate the premises at once or I may possibly never get out of there. In spotting a couple of good ol' drinking buddies from Klawock, I waved them over, pleading "You guys gotta help me with these drinks. Man I can't handle all these." Well now, bless their loving little hearts, they instantly obliged me as they pitched right in. With their baby-fingers crooked graciously, followed by a very pious expression upon their tanned and windblown features, downed five drinks apiece before I could even get off my stool and head for the door in order to find my New York cabbie.

What in blazes is this? I learned that Fred had already returned to Klawock and had no intention of returning to Craig until the following day because, as he put it, "I don't want to driving at night." I had no other choice but to start hiking the six miles back to Klawock. It wasn't until late that night, or was it early morning when I arrived back at the bunkhouse, thirsty, weary, fatigued and beat to the socks, where late the next day I received a whole lot of thank you's from those who had received some of the relaxing agent. I sure as heck didn't thank Fred in their behalf, believe me. And how was your Fourth of July? Whoopee!

ALL THAT GLITTERS

I'm afraid I'm guilty of painting a picture full of fun, excitement and beauty, but at the same time have failed to portray the other side of the picture. Yes, we too had our share of lawlessness and tragedies, the same as any accumulation of, what we call human beings had, whether it be in Timbuktu or Klawock. Therefore, I shall present an accumulation of these blots on an otherwise peaceful and friendly people, but shall soon return to a much nicer view on life in Alaska.

It wasn't really necessary that we venture forth from town to seek excitement when one could find it right in their own back yard. The evening that our school burned to the ground created enough excitement to last a lifetime.

Our school was an ancient wooden structure, two stories in heighth, with every inch of space being utilized from primer through Junior High. The floors throughout the building were also wooden, and the common practice for cleaning them was to give them a thorough sweeping, followed by mopping down with an oily mop which served to give them the appearance of being highly polished and sparkling clean. Ahem, some of the little first timers have been know to, when the urge is that great, whip out their teenie weenies from behind the back of a chair to contribute their own brand of polish to the floor. Also, due to an electrical overload, it was not too uncommon that the lights would at times black out. Likewise, it wasn't too uncommon that the janitor, or custodian as he liked to be called, rather than hunt down a fuse to replace the burned out one would insert a penny in its place. But by all means intended to rectify this, "Hey, don't ever do that," faux pa, at the earliest possible moment.

The town of Klawock had just recently qualified for a pair of ooh so pretty, beautiful red, Jeep Fire Engines, under the auspices of The Civilian Defense Program, which created as much furor and excitement throughout the village as Bailey's ass did in Craig. Practically everyone in town turned out to witness them being unloaded at the cannery dock, making quite a festive occasion of it. Eventually the Jeeps were stationed strategically along main street (the only street in town) all in readiness for whenever the fire alarm atop City Hall should scream for help.

A few weeks after the arrival of the Jeep fire engines, the school caught fire for a penny, the fire alarm screamed the news, while male villagers could be seen making a wild dash for the Jeeps. In the meantime the school presented those present with a spectacle unlike anything they'd ever witnessed before as the school turned into a raging inferno in a matter of minutes, especially with the help from the oil saturated floors. Due to the fact the structure was so very old and dry as a cob it took no more than thirty five minutes for the whole building to become nothing more than a pile of rubble, left smoldering on the ground.

I think I'm forgetting something? Well excuse me, I think I've failed to mention that both the fire Jeeps were dead in the water, as the expression goes. Someone of the local fishermen had elected to pirate the batteries from the Jeeps, but by all means intending to replace them at the earliest possible moment. The earliest possible moment never got there in time, so the school caught fire for a penny, and became totally obliterated for want of a battery. It isn't too hard to understand why I enjoyed getting out on the Harry, Jr. when you consider all the weird things associated with the human race.

For instance; Our little jailhouse in Klawock was another building that also caught fire and burned. The tribal police officer had thrown an inebriated Indian into the hoosegow that night, just like in the movies, ordering him to sleep it off for his own safety while fully intending to release him the following morning. Unfortunately while smoking, the poor prisoner set his mattress on fire causing the jail to burn big time. People passing by were unable to do a thing for him, poor soul, who by this time was hollering for his life at the top of his lungs. His cries for help were all in vain since the tribal officer was home in bed snoozing away with the keys to the jail snuggled tightly in his pants pocket. No jailer, no key, it was a tragedy void of all justice for the poor Indian who, unfortunately received the death sentence for no other reason than getting drunk.

Most of the bad happenings and deaths that occurred within our village can be attributed to the Indians reckless approach to drinking. The following story is no exception to the rule. However, I wish it to be understood that the greater majority of the Thlingets in our village drank moderately, if at all, and then only on special occasions. But as usual, there are always a few bad apples to spoil it for the rest. This is about them.

It was common talk about town that there were three old winos, who decided to manufacture a bit of booze on their own. Since Klawock was strictly a dry town they thought it would be too risky to mess with it in town, so they decided to set up their still on a neighboring island just across the bay from Klawock. They did eventually manage somehow to produce some white lightning, but it was next to impossible to keep it a secret. Every time they visited the island on the pretense of going fishing, they came back snockered. This prompted another old wino in town to launch a personal investigation of his own. Through sheer logic he was able to determine that in such a short interval between their going fishing and getting drunk it was not likely that they could have gone to Craig. Thereafter he kept a close watch on them and he soon discovered that their fishing trips always ended up at Wadleigh Island, only a mile across the bay from Klawock.

It didn't take long, however, for word to reach the three musketeers(winos) who owned the still, that another old wino was visiting Wadleigh Island on the sly, and appeared to be wearing a happy grin after each visit. They immediately took it upon themselves to set up a surveillance program of their own to determine how often and when the bootlegger, if you would call him that, raided their cache. They figured out a strategy, which entailed setting up an ambush to get this guy, when sure enough, he showed up just as they expected. When they popped up out of the brush to get him he was so taken by surprise he didn't have time to get to his skiff which was tied nearby. Instead, he leaped frantically into the water as a means to escape, whereas the three winos clambered into their own skiff and took off after him in hot pursuit.

The culprit stood not a chance of eluding his pursuers because of his being in the water. After a short and frantic sprint, he was forced to give up by reaching for the gunwales of their skiff in hopes they might drag him aboard for the beating he contemplated receiving. Rather than that one of the trio seized a hatchet and severed the hand. In agony and trying his best to survive, the victim once again reached for the side of the skiff, but once again the hatchet came into play, severing the other hand.

The Territorial Commissioner who was stationed in Craig at the time was serving on strictly a temporary basis, acting as a relief person for the regular Commissioner, Mrs Shroy, who was in Ketchikan on business for a few days. Our temporary Commissioner, a simple housewife, was appalled at the sight of blood, death or drownings, so without ever recovering the body or visiting the scene of the alleged confrontation, instead opted to issue a death certificate for the victim.

Cause of death! - - - Accidental drowning!

Such is life when dealing with the human element. I can offer you even more tragedies by following this vein of disclosure, but I'd much rather continue to show you an Alaska full of adventure, magic, and things to learn, about this vast territory as it used to was, but will never ever be that way again.

GAMBOLING THROUGH THE MUSKEGS

This chapter shall be dealing with a period in time when the new cannery in Klawock had completed a successful operation, and had then been laid up for the winter.

Isn't it wonderful that you can walk up to the sink, start the faucet and have all the water you wish. Not so in the wilderness area. Since we had a few stoppages during canning waiting for our water supply to build up, I received notice from the office in Seattle that I was to expect a shipment of pipe to arrive on the next ship making a trip to Alaska. I was further instructed to organize a crew of men from town to go up on the muskeg and replace any damaged or leaky pipes we could find. Fishing season was over so I had no trouble in organizing workers, since they were being offered an unexpected opportunity to earn some extra money.

After the ship arrived and delivered her load of pipe onto the dock, we made preparations to haul the stuff up to the muskegs and from there, go to work repairing the pipeline. Doesn't sound like too much of a job, right? Hah! The pipes come in ten, twelve, and fourteen-foot lengths. They are heavy wooden pipes eight inches in diameter, wrapped in heavy wire, then coated with layers of tar to protect them from the acidy soil common to the Muskeg.

"Muskeg," I wonder how many people fully understand the beginning of life for the Muskegs. Eons ago, the greater part of Alaska was a mass of nothing more than ice. Dust, dirt, and debris from the snow-melt on the higher levels seeped down onto any area that was flat enough to hold water and soil in amounts sufficient enough to provide nutrients where a seed deposited by the wind might flourish. Before long that seed shall produce a plant, while the plant in turn shall provide an additional amount of seeds, but more importantly shall deposit it's leaves onto the ice after shedding them in the fall, which in itself forms compost.. The continuation of this same procedure will produce more plants, more seeds, birds spreading seeds, compost being deposited over the ice, then also moss beginning to form.

There you have it, the Muskegs of Alaska are singularly unique in their composition of ice called Permafrost, lying in great depth beneath defoilated plant-life and moss, which eventually builds into a mat more than eighteen inches thick with no tap-roots of any kind to speak of. Unbelievably, with the coming of spring the muskegs burst forth with wild flowers, so suddenly and in such great profusion, it simply boggles the mind. There is nothing more beautiful than a muskeg when it is in full bloom, displaying an unprecedented array of brilliant and livid colors.

The pipe we must transport onto the muskegs have such a rough outer layer they cannot be carried comfortably upon your shoulders, so we came up with the idea of building several pair of yokes resembling the handles on a plow. The yolks were equipped with an extension in front that penetrated the pipe for a distance of 2-1/2 feet. Therefore, with a man at each end of a section of pipe and by inserting the yolk, he was afforded a practical method for transporting the pipe. The operation appeared to be like a Tarzan movie, as they usually exhibited a whole string of Natives in single file, packing huge bundles of equipment through the jungle. Our jungle was the Muskeg.

Eventually we managed to have everything in readiness to proceed with repairing leaks in the pipeline, and also replacing those that appeared to be doubtful. The work took several days to complete, so we had in our group an old timer who volunteered to be bull cook for the workers. His name was Harry Watson,

Sr. Unbelievably, he proved to be the best worker of all even though he was in his late seventies. My laying claim that our bull cook proved to be the best worker of all, shall prove to be the truth a bit later in the story.

We caulked the majority of small leaks with shingles and oakum, replaced a number of pipe sections, then happened upon the real culprit responsible for our shortage of water in the cannery. It was a section of pipe that had been ruptured by a huge boulder pushing upwards from the force of the ice below. After removing the damaged pipe and laying it aside, we were confronted with a real problem.

It turned out that the boulder was a lot bigger than we originally thought, but to make matters worse the damn thing was round as a billiard ball, affording us nary a hand hold or an irregular surface where we might get a grip on the thing. Picture six guys putting forth their greatest efforts all at the same time in an endeavor to roll the boulder out of the way, all to no avail. The rock was simply much too heavy, and slippery as well. Our next attempt at extracting the boulder was to cut several bull-pines to use as pry poles. In spite of having six men trying by prying, this proved to be equally as unsuccessful as all of our other efforts, since our prys sunk in the muck and the rock simply spun round like a beach ball.

Harry, the old timer, our bull cook had stood patiently by, observing our frantic antics, when he came forth to tap me on the shoulder. "Johnnie, it's better you take the crew home now. Then you come back for tomorrow, I gonna have the rock gone."

As always, I had learned to learn, rather than show my ignorance of this North Country, so I did as he advised by dismissing the crew for the time being. However, I was expecting them to return the following morning, while my mind was doing flip-flops in wondering if maybe poor ol' Harry had turned senile, and also if I were doing the right thing.

The following morning we all arrived at the job site to see Harry sitting atop a stack of extra pipe sections we had stored for future use. "Well I'll be damned," I muttered under my breath, because at the same time, I was completely flabbergasted in spotting the offensive boulder lying off to one side, with nothing more than a gaping hole showing where it had so recently occupied space.

I was fairly bursting to know how this was accomplished, but etiquette you know, the Indian way demanded that I wait for a respectable interval of time, allowing for the old fella to enjoy the moment before I meandered over to sit beside him and exchanged greetings. "Wasaw Eh Teewhanee, (hope things are going well for you this morning) Konash Chees, Johnnie, (Thank you) Finally, it was time, so I inquired. "Okay, Harry, how'd ya do it?" Flashing a grin as broad as a horse eating thistles, Harry countered with, "Johnnie, I seen that rock is too slippery. Then I seen the poles sink when you try to pry this rock out from the ground. I got some seal meat hung up under the house, and I seen all dis skunk cabbage he's being dug up everywhere. Dis is why I gone home for the seal meat to bury it under the rock." "Come look."

He pointed to a rash of claw marks all around the outer surface of the boulder. "See, I knowed dis is a bear tored up all the skunk cabbage. They eat the roots before they go to sleep. I already know the bear is going to get that seal meat out cause he is very strong that bear, so that is why he got the rock out."

It certainly would have been a most interesting show had I been there to witness the monster in action as he worked to extract the boulder and claim his prize. The bear no doubt demonstrated an unparalleled combination of power, and dogmatic tenacity to finally gain that one chunk of meat.

Oh, I nearly forgot. I'm almost certain I told you the old man did more work than the others, did I not? +

A FISH GAVE ME THE BIRD

During the time when I was in Craig making an ass of myself, (hauling oil drums on a hand cart) didn't allow me much time for fun stuff. Now that I'd become settled in Klawock and had a bit more time to myself, I decided to take on the mighty King, electing to work the Craig-Klawock channel since I was advised it was good King Salmon country. The channel was conveniently located just a short distance straight out from my home, offering me quick access to a popular fishing area.

There I was, all decked out with the white mans idea of perfect fishing gear when I was accosted by one of the local boys, Harry Watson, Jr, who advised me to chuck the junk, then proceeded to show me how to create a sure fire lure.

"Okay, we take this herring, then we cut it in half like this." (He fileted the herring) Now you gonna strip the meat from the one whole side to leave a chunk of meat just big enough to set the hook in it, okay?" He tossed me the other half of the filet to be used as a spare and away I went.

All excited like, I ventured forth with a super strong salmon rod sporting one whopping mammoth sized Penn reel loaded to the n'th with 2500 ft of 27lb test, monofilament line. In addition to this I had taken extra precautions that should I manage to snag a King he would most assuredly not escape, by further attaching a stainless steel leader to the end of my line. After all this clever preparation I was more than confident everything was in readiness for anything ol' Mr King Salmon might throw at me.

I was thinking how nice it would be to have a nice smooth running and dependable outboard motor pushing me along. I was that anxious to try my new lure.

Rather than that, It was my lot to be running about in an old outmoded, noisy 9.75 H.P. long shanked Johnson outboard motor, fastened onto the transom of my beat-up and ugly looking fourteen foot skiff. (so?) This is the kind of equipment the Indians use and they sure as hell catch fish, so what's the problem?

Minutes later, upon making my landing and securing the skiff, I scampered up onto some large boulders jutting into the channel, and got all set to cast for Kings with my magical lure.

Man oh man, talk about magical. I had no more than flipped the herring out when WHAMO!, something hit that lure so hard I was convinced I had hooked onto a seal, or maybe a whale, or maybe even a rabid log, when within seconds following the strike there was a spine tingling roar from behind as an Eagle swooped down to snag my catch, raising it swiftly from the water. It was plain to see that both an Eagle and I had caught a beautiful king-sized, King Salmon. Most generally when you spot an Eagle, he's sitting high atop an old snag, appearing to be the size of a banty hen. Therefore, I was aghast by the size of this huge bird swooping down, hardly more than 50 ft from my nose, aghast at the size of the fish he elected to carry off, and I ghast I'd better do something much pronto, or end up being aghast again from losing all my gear.

I've now come to the conclusion that this could prove to be a real challenge. The Eagle's hooked onto my salmon, the salmons hooked onto my gear, and the whole kit and kaboodle is skyward bound heading for who knows where. After my initial fright caused by the Eagles mind boggling strike, I had the prescence of mind to tighten the drag on my reel a bit at a time. This brilliant maneuver increased the resistance for the Eagle, who by this time was showing signs of tiring due to the drag of my line.

Gradually, the fish and bird combo came about in a long sweeping arc, actually heading back towards me. Meanwhile my line had been playing out at an alarming rate until that time when the bird started it's arc, causing me to crank like a mad man in order to salvage my line and to take up the slack. Wow! what a situation to be in. Eventually the bird became increasingly more tired and continued to lose altitude, until that time when it's wings touched down into the water enabling the salmon to drag the bird beneath the surface and so drowned the Eagle. I had no recourse other than to keep on reeling in this soggy conglomerate consisting of a huge fish and a huge bird in order that I might salvage my gear.

I had no idea as to what in the world to do with the Eagle. However upon my arrival back in Klawock, my struggle had been witnessed from town, so the kids were all over me, excitedly proclaiming me, "Mighty Hunter." (Yaash Koo Whooh) The little devils, because of my pointed nose they called me Yaash Koo Whooh, which I found out later means, "CROW'S NOSE"

It became necessary to carve a chunk out of the salmon in order to extract the Eagles talons, as they were interlocked and firmly imbedded in its back. After freeing the salmon someone volunteered a hand-held scale whereas we were able to determine the fish weighed in at 38 lbs. Now that is a lot of weight in any mans language for a bird to attempt to carry off. Nevertheless, I was advised the bird could in fact carry more weight than that, if it hadn't been entangled in my gear.

Soon afterward the kids were holding the Eagle spread-eagled in order to take pictures, and also to measure the birds wingspread which proved to be just over seven feet in width. A mighty big bird. I wondered aloud why the Eagle hadn't simply dropped the fish rather than get it'self drowned. The old timers claimed that once an Eagle latches onto it's prey with the talons interlocked, it is not likely that it will disengage them until that time when it can set down to rid itself of the weight, and for this reason the Eagle was drowned.

Time and distance intervened. I thought I might get into the Guiness World Book of Records. After all, how many others have caught a 38 lb Salmon, and a 7 ft bird with one flip of a herring?

A TYPICAL CANNING SEASON

It is usually late June when the salmon runs begin in S. E. Alaska. This heralds a period in time when all our concentrated pre-season preparations suddenly become secondary in scope as the first load of salmon arrives at the cannery. There is an air of excitement in witnessing thousands of salmon being delivered onto the fish elevator, a continuous chain of buckets, which transport the salmon up and into the cannery. As soon as they enter the cannery the salmon are deposited upon a large rubber conveyor belt running from one end of a series of storage bins, to the other, where they are sorted according to species. ie; Sockeye (red salmon) are all stored in one bin, then Coho (medium red salmon) frequently referred to as silvers, in another, followed by Humpies (pink salmon) and finally Dog salmon, commercially defined as either Chum or Ketah, depending on the area in which they were being utilized.

Step up to the sorting belt with me and marvel at the ability of the Filipino sorters in separating, and extracting the various species of Salmon as they come down the conveyor belt, piled high on top of one another. It is am amazing fete. Although only a very small part of any one fish might be showing, the sorters nevertheless, are able to identify immediately and accurately, from a fin, a tail or even a nose, protruding from the heap. Thus a hint no matter how minute enables them to extract that fish and steer it into the proper bin for processing the following day.

From the holding bins let us follow as the salmon begin their journey toward the finished product as they are by being directed into a machine called the Iron

Chink. Here they are beheaded and gutted, with the tails and fins removed all in the same operation. The "Chink" as it is called, is capable of performing this task at the rate of 55 fish per minute. From the "Chink" the Salmon are passed onto a conveyer belt, where they are inspected and cleansed of any foreign matter the chink had failed to remove. From this point they are transferred into the filler machines for their final journey into the cans, where they shall then be weighed, sealed, and cooked. This phase of the operation is really something to witness. The salmon are fed into the filler machine whole, (in the round is actually the proper term for the salmon at this stage) while from another source but at the same time, the filler machine is being fed with a continual chain of empty cans. It is imperative that the empty cans be positioned directly under the plunger as it forces exactly one pound of salmon into their gaping bodies. Amazingly this process is being accomplished at the rate of 242 cans per minute.

From here let us follow the salmon all snug in their wee little cans as they are weighed precisely within an eighth of an ounce to make certain they contain a full pound of salmon. A machine called a clincher slaps on a cover bearing a code, which defines the date they were processed, the cannery from which the fish originated, besides identifying the specie of fish within the can. Following this procedure, the cans, still moving along at 242 cans a minute, are run through a series of vacuum seamers. This machine removes every trace of outside air from within the can while at the same time enjoins the lid to the can with a double rolled seam, guaranteeing an airtight seal.

Huge steam cookers defined as retorts are awaiting the finished product. The canned salmon shall be subjected to a temperature in excess of 240 degrees for a period of 90 minutes at 11 lbs. pressure, assuring that the fish shall be thoroughly cooked to the extent that the bone is as soft as the rest of the salmon.

So there you have it. I hope I've managed to enlighten you as to how the salmon are processed. The cannery could normally process in excess of 50,000 salmon per day when employing but one canning line. However, in the early 1900's when the salmon runs were unbelievably bountiful, multiple canning lines were put into operation in many of the canneries throughout Southeastern Alaska. As is always the case, because of man's natural greed for the almighty dollar, the massive salmon runs of yesteryear were eventually depleted, forcing the canneries to consolidate and reduce their operations to a single canning line.

Mankind sure is a dumb-bunny sometimes, right?

LIVERING IT UP

A lot of you readers will no doubt wonder why I even brought this subject up, but it does contain some very interesting points, and that is the main reason for my writing it. If I failed to enlighten you on all aspects of this Alaska adventure, I would feel that I had gypped you out of learning something you may not have been aware of, so here goes, let's have fun while we learn about liver.

What in the world possesses a man, who, although he isn't even pregnant, suddenly develops an overwhelming desire for a liver dinner?

It was inevitable that I did eventually satisfy this indescribable craving by discovering the most tender, the most flavorful and finest liver known to man. Believe it or not, I am referring to one that is superior even to deer liver, and that is hard to beat. I didn't think you would come up with the right answer. It's seal liver!

It may shock you to find a seal's liver to be equally as large as a beef liver, and while the beef liver has tough cords running throughout, I promise you, never will you encounter a cord whatsoever hiding within a tender and succulent seal liver. Now, in addition to this, one might expect to discover somewhat of a fishy taste associated with the seal liver, but quite contrary to this belief you would discover a seal liver to be as odorless as a wee baby's bottom. (at certain times) Okay, now hold on a second and I'll tell you how I learned all this stuff.

The majority of you readers have probably never tasted seal liver due to the fact that it is extremely hard to come by. Permit me then to expostulate on my very first seal hunt, strictly on my own. I'd gone over to Esquable channel to try for a seal. After having beached the skiff and gone ashore I spotted a group of hair seals cavorting in the water about 150 yds ahead of me. After belly-whopping painfully over some rocky terrain, I assumed a position where I could observe the seals without being seen. However, I had also assumed a position where there were several damnably sharp rocks stabbing into my guts from various angles beneath my body. Aha! I've aimed the sights on my trusty 30-30 Winchester rifle in perfect alignment onto the head of a seal protruding above the water. Ooh, both my elbow and my ribs are pleading, "C'mon man, get the damned shot off before we start bleeding," but they were too late with their sniveling demands, I had already squeezed back on the trigger. After three more similar attempts, but having no more satisfaction than witnessing a lil' poof where the bullet had struck the water, I was forced to give up and acknowledge that my trusty ol' 30-30 was Kaput! I was certain it had to be the gun because I knew I had the blankety blank seal dead in my sights before I fired.

So, back at the Bar-S ranch as the saying goes, I encountered my good Indian friend, Fred Anniskette, who had just turned 73 years old. Upon burdening Fred with a rendition on my inability to nail a seal, even after adjusting my sights a number of times, he set me straight by offering me some solid information. Fred was definitely all Indian, so he spoke like this. "Johnnie, I seen you have this 30-30. No good that one." "Johnnie, I know dese seals. When you shoot the seal from the rock where they sleepin, they gonna sink, cause from the rock to the water when they falling, they blow out the air from the lungs, so this is gonna make them sink. You must got to hit them when they are in the water, wasaw?"

Fred continued, hanging onto each word as though he was pondering how to tell me, "Johnnie, with the 30-30 you got there, he didn't miss the seal, the seal miss the bullet." Oh, oh, I've got to wait this one out. Fred then motioned for me to follow as he led me to a shed in his yard. He quickly extracted a rather small looking rifle from a gun rack mounted on the wall. "Dis the one shoots the seal," he exclaimed. "This is only two guns like this one. Mine is the 218B. The nother one from Winchester, they call it the 222." Fred pointed out that it had an oversized magazine which was especially designed to accommodate a much larger casing than a regular 22 rifle, thus a shot fired from these two particular models traveled at an accelerated speed many times faster than an ordinary shell.

Fred offered further. "Johnnie, that 30-30 you got. The bullet goes slow but the noise goes fast, so when you shooted at the seal he hears the bang noise before the bullet gets there, so now he goes under the water and misses the bullet, wasaw? (you understand) "Now he don't heard the noise from this one, Johnnie," Fred continued as he held the 218B aloft. "When you see the seal, dis means he is full of air cause you wouldn't seen him if he was sunk." "When you shoot the seal dis time with that one," Once more the 218B was held aloft as he emphasized his point, "He won't sink down because he is too dead to blow out the air from his body, okay?"

Fred hesitated as though pondering a problem, then announced, "Johnnie, I want for you to put dis one in you head. I know that seal. When he go down by heself, you look at you watch. He goes down for three minutes then always come up close to that same place. Remember, always he goes down three minutes, okay?" Then in response to his having pondered over a problem, Fred offered, "Here, you take this gun and try like I told you," as he handed me his rifle plus a handful of the special shells. "You gonna be smart Indian." "Konas Chees. (thank you) my friend," I replied.

Consequently I managed to bag a seal the following morning, so when returning the rifle and the unspent shells to their rightful owner, I made certain they were accompanied by a nice chunk of seal liver. Fred accepted the rifle but not the liver, simply stating, "We don't eat that one." He closed the door and I somehow got the feeling I had been dismissed. Another lesson, a renewal of trust in my trusty 30-30, but most importantly, a stronger bond between my Indian tutor, and myself.

Incidentally, you may be wondering, since Fred did not eat liver why would he possess a special seal rifle. Before Alaska became a State, all Alaska's residents were offered two dollars apiece for a hair seals nose. The seals were destroying spawning salmon by the hundreds, simply by biting the bellies out of the salmon, then leaving the rest of the fish untouched. So consequently there were several 218B's and 222's within the village.

A LEGEND IN HIMSELF

We had in our village an old timer named Charlie Demmert. This guy was a real character, believe me. Charlie was 65 yrs. old when I first met him, a big man who weighed 225 lbs. and had a 225 lb. voice to go with it. He walked with a cane due to the fact that he was at this stage in life, arthritic, and had slowed down to the point where he used a chair as a prop while conducting any form of activity outside of heckling someone or another. In spite of all this Charlie was still a doer in every sense of the word, one who was especially noted for his uncanny ability to move houses or buildings with some of the most decrepit and antiquated pieces of equipment known to man.

Included in his outmoded, though useful inventory, was an old pile driver mounted on a log raft, and with this disheveled contraption sitting on moss covered and half submerged logs, did manage to drive piling, then would miraculously end up placing a building on top of the piling.

Charlie as a rule, used native help during his pile driving operations, preferably a couple of old drunks, since they would work for very little pay and with the thought in mind they might throw a little party later on, if you know what I mean. On this particular day Charlie had two of the boys working for him on the driver. There he sat, spraddle-legged on his chair while leaning forward on his cane with a huge chunk of his belly bulging forth, no doubt seeking support from any source whatsoever, but in vain. Charlie liked this position in the galley since the walls and studs, well in fact the whole front end of the structure was non-existent, thus affording him an unobstructed view in all directions. Well now, right in front of where Charlie was sitting there's a trap door in the floor which was put to use in disposing of leftover food, too many hotcakes, poor cooks, whatever, down the hatch.

Charlie had a great sense of humor and was more than eager to display it as long as it was at the expense of the other party. First you must envision him, spread out on his little chair like the reigning Sultan from Arabia, as he suddenly bent forward to yank open the trap door at his feet. While feigning a look of alarm he bellowed, "Boys, boys, come quick, the barge is sinking," as he pointed alarmingly at the open trap door where the water was plainly visible just inches from the floor.

Both his helpers charged helter-skelter to grab buckets, and commenced bailing like mad. Charlie watched concernedly for a brief period of time, then gradually sat back as though he felt everything was under control at this point. After a brief, though frantic effort to reduce the level of the water, one of the two helpers casually walked over to grab a chair and joined Charlie. His partner gallantly increased his efforts to keep the driver afloat when, "BOING!" the light went on for him, also.

At this moment Charlie could contain himself no longer and broke out into a boisterous fit of laughter as the two helpers came to the realization they had been had. Of course there was no way they could possibly have reduced the level of the water, simply because the driver was sitting on a log raft, whereas the water level was already determined by how low in the water the logs allowed the driver to sit.

I would like also to mention that, in his hey-day Charlie was one rugged hunk of man. With all of his 225 lbs., and standing better than six feet tall, quite naturally he had an attitude equal to these gargantuan proportions. Thus, when Charlie went on a hunting spree he didn't elect to settle for just one deer, but would instead bag three or four at the same time, then he proceed to relay them back to the village all by himself. At the time this incident took place, Charlie had managed to bag four deer up on the muskegs above Klawock Creek about a quarter mile from the town of Klawock. During the act of relaying the deer towards home he had managed to attract a pack of wolves. Quite naturally the wolves moved in swiftly to start devouring his kill.

Charlie immediately counter charged into them, waving his arms and yelling, "Get the Hell outa here, ya damn mangy scavengers." He would then grab two deer at a time and relay them some distance homeward, only to return and find the pack intent on the two remaining deer. Again he would drive them off, yelling obscenities and waving his rifle high in the air. Once again he would continue to relay the deer farther towards town until that time when he had all four deer close enough to the village where the wolves finally drew back, leaving the victor the spoils.

One day I confronted Charlie to question him about this encounter. "Why?" I asked, hadn't he fired his rifle, while at the same time arguing that he must surely have put himself in jeopardy in view of the fact that the wolf pack had gotten the scent of blood. His only comment was, "There was only a dozen of them, and I wasn't about to waste a bullet on them, nor was I going to give that good meat to them damn mongrels."

As I mentioned previously, Charlie had a great sense of humor, but while gazing upon his stern features during this portion of our discussion, I felt certain he was not humoring me at all.

One day I happened upon Charlie in a discussion with one of his Indian laborers who by all accounts appeared to be slightly hung over. There was no doubt that this Indian fella was becoming mighty dry, because under normal circumstances he would never consider asking Charlie for money, but in times of dire need he was somewhat bolstered to confront the big man and inform him. "Charlie, you owe me for four hours." "I do? You sure about that?" Charlie responded in a very gruff manner, while at the same time winked at me. Oh! Oh! I was instantly alerted that Charlie was going to get something going. I waited patiently for whatever was to develop from their conversation.

"Charlie, you remember I worked from last Saturday, I didn't get paid for it," was the immediate rebuttal. Following a long pause while Charlie did some mental calculating, he grudgingly conceded that the Indian laborer could be right. "Okay, I owe you for four hours," he replied, indignantly. "You can come to work tomorrow and I let you work it off, Okay?" The Indian responded with a sigh of relief that this had gone over so easily, "Okay, I'll be here tomorrow from 9:00 O'clock." Then he turned and literally scooted outa there, no doubt feeling proud that he had braved the wrath of the man and had escaped unharmed.

I was dumbfounded! Did I hear right? Did this conversation actually take place? But for sure, I was dere Sharlie and heard the whole thing. Charlie merely laughed, saying, "Don't worry, he'll catch on later, but by then it will be too late for him to do anything about it today, he just gets nervous about confronting me." "I thought it was best he sober up, so I stalled him off." Charlie then turned to laboriously make his way up the flight of stairs leading to his house. Just for a moment I thought I heard a bird, then realized it could have just as easily been Charlie, the tough old bird, chuckling to himself.

INTENSE WAS THE BATTLE

Being in the right place at the right time oft times results in your witnessing an extremely rare incident or an unbelievably exciting event. The story we are about to share tops this, and is without doubt a once in a lifetime experience.

My native fishing companion, whose name was Harry Watson Jr., and I, had just entered Esquibal Channel, where we had made fast onto a large boulder in order that we might have a bite to eat. Our snack consisted of a nice big tasty chunk of dried halibut and some pilot bread. Here in Alaska nearly everyone used pilot bread rather than real bread since bread was a luxury, beside the fact that it got stale or moldy right away. On the other hand Pilot bread was already stale to tell the truth, because it consisted of nothing more than an unsalted, oversized soda cracker that had been compressed, then kiln dried in order to preserve it.

Our position atop the huge boulder afforded us a grandiose view of the surrounding channel, when Harry made an observation. "Sure a bunch of killer whales around right now, must be because it is mating time for the big ones." I assumed he was referring to the numerous gray whales and humpbacks we were witnessing from time to time.

The Orca are called killer whales by the Thlingets here in S,E. Alaska, because they are noted for hunting in packs of six or seven just like "Wolves of the Sea". In fact from our vantage point high upon the rock, we were able to observe a number of Orca traversing the channel directly in front of where we were seated. It was a very clear day so the Orca were outstanding in their beautiful markings of black and white, their huge dorsals protruding from the water at different intervals as though regimented by an unseen source demanding, "Up Periscope." Suddenly, as though by command, they altered their pace from that smooth and leisurely roll we were accustomed to seeing, into one of haste and intent. The reason for their sudden activity was not long in presenting itself.

In the channel, and directly in front of the Orca, a large gray whale appeared. It soon became apparent that the pack of Orca seemed intent on overtaking the whale. This proved to be true, when in a matter of minutes they had actually come upon the monstrous creature to immediately launch an attack. Normally, the killer whale will select the hair seal as it's favorite food, oft times snagging them while they are swimming about in the water. However, they are not above dragging them off the ice floes during the winter when everything is frozen solid and the seals are lying around on the ice, sunning themselves and primping. This is the time when the seal is most vulnerable to an attack from a killer whale. An Orca cruises the outer edge of the ice floe until that time when he spots a seal close to the edge. He immediately launches his massive frame up onto the ice as smoothly as an ice skater, then clamps onto the seal as he slides back into the water with his prey grasped firmly in those unrelenting jaws.

In the meantime, the gray whale had turned about to face it's adversaries and was fast heading our way rewarding us with a graphic view of its doing battle with the attacking killer whales. What a terrifying sight as the Orca could be observed darting in and out towards the whale's head, biting chunks of flesh from it's jowls, causing the water surrounding the battle area to become frothy and pink. At times the whale would come boiling straight up out of the water, appearing like an apartment house, while at the same time the Orca would rise right with it, clinging onto the whales cheeks.

What a nerve shattering sight this battle presented to Harry and I, as we watched, totally awestruck by the ferocity of the attack on the whale. I wondered aloud that the killer whales could subdue such a monstrous creature as the whale, when by comparison, the Orca appeared to be no larger than one of the flukes on this denizen of the deep.

Of course, in a place such as Sea World where you are afforded the opportunity to come face to face with the Orca, the Orca appears to be as large as a dirigible. Out here in the broad expanse of the ocean, they appeared to be no larger than a minnow as they were being suspended in mid-air on the cheeks of this huge whale.

The whale continued to boil up out of the water a few more times, while each time shaking it's massive head frantically in an endeavor to dislodge the Orca clinging to it's cheeks. At the same time it would twist and arch it's body in an attempt to land upon any one of the attacking killer whales. Harry and I watched spellbound at the amazing spectacle taking place before our very eyes, as the water surrounding the battlefield became even more red and frothy from the incessant thrashing of that massive gray body, combined with the blood dripping from it's lacerated jowls. I'm sure Harry was sweating as profusely as I over the fate of the humpback whale, when suddenly we both let out a big war whoop because, believe it or not, the injured whale had managed to land squarely on top of one of it's attackers. Then just as suddenly as you snap your fingers, everything was still.

I was completely dumbfounded. "What the heck," I exclaimed! "What happened?" "Johnnie," Harry explained, with a slight accent. "I heard it before, these killer whales can't beat up the big whale like in a real fight. They gonna tease the big one from biting his cheeks, what makes the whale so tired he's gonna pant like the dog. When this happens the killer whale bites off the tongue from the big whale to make him drowned, then comes the Orca from all over and they have a feast like a pack of wolves. That's where the Thlingets call Orca the Sea Wolves." "Anyway," he continued, "The big whale won this time. You seen when the big whale landed on the other one, the Orca. He falls on top of that big fin standing up, to drive it down into the killer whale just like a spear. That is what happened. So now the rest of the pack goes after the hurted killer whale and let the big guy go."

"Woosh!" After witnessing an encounter as savage as this, I no longer envision Namu, and the likes of him at Sea World, to be those obedient and beautiful black and white pets, so willing to bow to mans whim. Rather than that, I'm thinking. "Just let ol' Namu spot you in the waters of Alaska, and he'd more than likely, damn well have your waggin tongue."

FUN FISHING OR DISASTER

There is nothing can compare to the excitement you experience when you're out fishing and hook onto a big one. Well these guys glommed onto a big one sure enough. How they managed to drag it aboard in the first place is beyond my comprehension.

It was customary for the cannery to employ a crew of Filipino workers from Stateside at the start of the fishing season. These were the same migratory workers that followed the crops throughout California. At certain seasons they would be picking celery, then tomatoes and lettuce, etc. After their arrival in Klawock there was a period of time covering a week or so before the cannery got into full swing, leaving the Filipinos at loose ends, more or less just kinda milling about the grounds of an evening while becoming orientated with their new surroundings. Filipinos are notably very fond of fish, so in discovering there were schools of shiners, little guys that resembled crappies, in the harbor directly in front of the cannery, they became excited over the prospect of catching some of them. Since they were well acquainted with me from previous contacts, they immediately sought me out and pleaded with me to help them to go fishing.

Beached on the beach was an old double ended skiff belonging to my friend, Isaac Katasse, who willingly gave us permission to use it providing we should first recaulk it and make it seaworthy once more. Duck soup! Early Saturday morning there were at least 15 inexperienced Filipino volunteers, swarming all over a twelve foot skiff, some energetically pounding cotton into the seams, while others were just as enthusiastically scraping the hull in preparation for painting. It became mandatory that one had to be especially alert when wielding a hammer, simply because there were so many hands in the pie, and that resulted in, if you did happen to hit a finger more than likely it would prove to be someone's other than your own. Do not doubt for one second, that should this happen, there would most certainly be a very noticeable increase in the volume of yipping and yapping already in effect. It was really something to witness. Unbelievably, the poor little skiff was so covered with workers it was difficult to determine whether it was six, eight, or ten of the little guys, who were busily swinging brushes filled with paint, half on themselves and half on the hull.

In addition to that, they were chattering like magpies, creating a din that could be heard all over the cannery premises. If you'll stop for a moment and visualize a schoolyard full of happy kidlets having recess, you'll then see the picture.

By the end of the day, I had to admit the little skiff looked mighty pretty, all clean and freshly painted by the time this horde of ants was through with it, although I most assuredly could not say the same for the Filipinos. Whoever is of the opinion that the modern day high school youth invented painted hair. WRONG!

The following morning early, which was on a Sunday, five zealous Filipino fishermen had been launched and sent abroad upon the briny deep. Within an hour's time just a short distance out from the cannery they could be observed hauling in shiners like mad, whooping excitedly over each and every conquest.

It so happened that I was standing on the cannery float, appreciative of the fact they were being happily rewarded for all their effort in fixing up the skiff. Then all of a sudden their happy little yips and yaps took on an entirely different tone. Something apparently had gone wrong. They appeared to be standing on the seats, jumping about as though something was inside the boat frightening them. Very soon thereafter, I came to the realization that their skiff was sinking, and that a few of the Filipinos were actually in the water. I immediately commandeered one of our power skiffs tied nearby, then rushed out to where they were fishing. Before I could reach them the rest of them were also in the water and the skiff was nearly half sunk. Fortunately they had the presence of mind to cling to the sides of the skiff for the short time it took me to get to them. I then commenced doing some fishing of my own by yanking them out of the water in the same manner as a fish, bug-eyed, wet and cold.

The cause of all the trouble stemmed from their having hooked onto a large halibut. Unfortunately they had managed to drag it into the boat with them, totally unaware of the fact that a halibut is one powerful fish. Any halibut will thrash about savagely when raised from the water, and is capable of pounding the bottom out of a small boat should you fail to bash him in the head the moment you've brought him aboard. Believe you me, I took care of that little project the moment I arrived on the scene by clubbing their catch into submission with a stunning blow between the eyes with a gaff hook we always carried in each power skiff. That alleviated any further disaster from his thrashing about.

We were very fortunate that this little sojourn into the briny deep turned out to be a laugh story rather than a tragic one, to hear them while chattering wildly, relive the incident. So in spite of their harrowing experience the whole Filipino crew was justifiably rewarded with their favorite dish, fish and rice.

It is my personal opinion that in addition to their halibut feast, they were equally rewarded with a hair raising true Alaskan adventure they would be more than eager to recount to the folks back home, or for that matter, anyone who would be willing to listen.

HEY, ANYBODY GOT A BATTERY

It really wasn't necessary that we venture forth from town to have exciting things happen here in Klawock. The evening that our schoolhouse burned to the ground created enough excitement to last everyone a lifetime.

Our school consisted of an old wooden structure dating back to the time when Ponce De Leone found out Christopher Columbus was going to discover America, so he decided to discover the Fountain of Youth to even the score. Of course this is nothing more than hearsay, so suit yourselves if you choose to accept this, or not.

Incidentally, the floors throughout our school building were made entirely of wood. The common practice for cleaning them was to first sweep them thoroughly with a broom, followed by a good going over with a mop impregnated with a special oil, The oil served to give the floors a sparkling clean, and highly polished appearance. The structure was two stories high with every classroom being utilized from primary through Junior High. Due to this overload, it was not too uncommon that the lights would, at times, black out. Likewise, it wasn't too uncommon that the janitor-custodian, rather than hunt down a fuse to replace the burned out one would instead insert a penny in its place. But of course, and by all means, intending to alter this most hazardous condition at the earliest possible moment.

The town of Klawock had just recently qualified for a pair of ooh, so pretty, beautiful red Jeep fire engines under the Civilian Defense Program, which created as much furor and excitement in the village, as did Bailey's ass when it landed in Craig. In fact, the whole town turned out to witness them being unloaded at the cannery dock, making a festive occasion of their arrival. Eventually the Jeeps were stationed strategically along Main street, which happened to be the only street in town, all in readiness for that time when the air raid siren atop the City Hall should scream for help.

No more than a few weeks following the arrival of the Jeep fire engines, the schoolhouse caught fire for a penny, the siren screamed the news, and a number of volunteers could be seen making a wild dash for the Jeeps. In the meantime, the schoolhouse presented those who were present with a present unlike any other, as the building turned into a raging inferno, especially with the help from the oil saturated floors. Due to the fact that the structure was very, very old, dry as a cob, and wooden from top to bottom, it took less than thirty five minutes for it to be reduced to a pile of rubble and hot coals, lying smoldering on the ground.

I have this strange feeling, like somehow I'm forgetting something. Well excuse me, I believe I've failed to mention that both of those beautiful, bright red Jeep fire engines were dead in the water, as the expression goes. Someone of the local fishermen had elected to pirate the batteries from the Jeeps, but of course, and by all means intending to replace them at the earliest possible moment. Unfortunately, the earliest possible moment failed to get there in time, so the school caught fire for a penny, then became totally obliterated for want of a battery. With such goings on going on, honestly now, can you blame me for looking forward to shipping out on the Harry, Jr. now and then?

INDIAN FOOD GOOD

Due to the advent of fine highways, fast trucks, and the airplane, plus super markets in some of the larger towns, it has become a simple task to purchase staples like bread, milk, eggs, etc. Have you ever stopped to consider how the pioneer Alaskans managed to survive without these modern conveniences in years gone by.

I know it's true, Alaska doesn't have a very long summer in which to grow crops, Nevertheless, you may be surprised to find how many natural foods there are to be found here in S. E. Alaska, and easily accessible to those knowledgeable enough to capitalize on their abundance.

When we do get the sun, it's for sixteen, eighteen, or even twenty hours a day, causing plant life to progress at a tremendous rate. Plants pop up out of the ground seemingly overnight, heralding the news there shall be a bumper crop of berries, rhubarb, goosetongue, wild cranberries, and even Hudson's Bay tea. All these goodies suddenly appear like magic and in large quantities, either to be canned or dried in preparation for another winter's arrival.

Hey, how'dja like to indulge in some soap berry ice cream. These little red berries, maybe twice the size of a B-B are the kid's favorite treat. All you have to do is place no more than six or seven of these tiny, fleshy, pericarped seeds, into a large, and I mean a very large bowl, whip'em up and you'll be amazed to discover what appears to be a huge bowl of frothy soap suds. Aha! Not so. These frothy suds when sprinkled with nothing more than good old C & H, pure cane sugar from Hawaii, magically become "Indian Ice Cream." It is really amusing to observe the Indian kids having fun guzzling this stuff, smacking their lips and laughing gleefully while they compete in capturing the bubbly suds without becoming inundated in the process. I'd say it was kind of like the kids Stateside, eating cotton candy, but in a more reckless and carefree manner. Enough of the soap opera, hi ho, hi ho, it's back to food we go.

The sea is far more bountiful than the land in providing the native population with food fare because it offers a continuous harvest rather than a seasonal one.

The advent of winter must always be taken into consideration, so the natives prepare well in advance of its inevitable arrival. Thus red snapper, several species of cod, herring, trout, salmon and halibut are put up and preserved, either through a smoking or drying process. Once any one of these sea-foods are dried, it is a simple matter to hang them on a beam or any place where they will stay dry. If no moisture is allowed to get to them they will keep for an indefinite period of time.

Thus, when preparing the dried fish to be served as a meal, all one has to do is steam them mildly, which tends to bring them back to their original consistency. Following this regenerating process, it is common practice that the fish be broken up into small pieces then sprinkled over steamed rice which has already been Impregnated with butter and soy sauce. Now, as a final gourmet touch, over the top of this savory concoction feel free to sprinkle an ample amount of dried seaweed, which adds a flavor unmatched by any other garnish known to man.

If you were a true Thlinget, you would cover your rice dish with either Naas grease (the Indian name for oulicon oil,) or herring oil. Each is equally delicious although, since the herring is so plentiful in comparison to the oulicon, the herring oil is more commonly put to use. (the oulicon is similar to the grunyon that inhabits the beaches in California at certain tides.)

As you can see there is constantly a wide selection of plant life and seafood available to the inhabitants of this well provisioned land, Alaska, and I haven't even mentioned clams, crab, octopus, lady slippers, and gum-boots.

We even find healing, bi-products at our fingertips. In fact I'd like to introduce you to a couple of them, okay?

You should by all means have some of this in your medicine cabinet. The Indians name it, "Gink" or "Stink heads" It is nothing more than dog salmon heads, placed in a burlap bag weighted down with rocks, then strategically set out on the beach so that the tide covers it when incoming, but exposes it when receding. This process must go on for a period of eight to ten days, or at least until that time when the fish heads become so rotten that the flesh will just plain fall from the skull. This is when you may reap your reward.

After the meat has been shaken free of the skull, directly behind each eye socket shall be exposed a small piece of gristle. It is cherry pink in color and somewhat transparent, besides bearing an odor of extremely rotten fish, that when one smells it they will be thoroughly convinced what they are smelling is indeed, stinking rotten fish. C'mon gang, don't give up on me. Pleease! read on.

Robert Snook, a Shaman, along with Spencer Williams, also a Shaman, will swear that eating a chunk of "Gink" will prevent anyone from getting a bad cold, "Like the flu gives you," as they so amply put it.

I actually had the opportunity to confront several doctors about this strange belief, and they concurred that what the Indians claimed, was true. They offered that penicillin was derived from mould, so what could more likely be penicillin than "Gink?" The Shamen certainly had no knowledge of penicillin other than "Gink" cured colds and flu. Strange isn't it that they uncovered pure penicillin from employing this unorthodox procedure. Stranger still is the fact that only the dog salmon heads bear this small piece of gristle. It surely makes one wonder what sense of reasoning caused them to engage in such an ungodly practice in the first place.

Damn, lest I forget, I wanted to inform you of the manner in which the "Gink" is administered. ie; "Pinch your nose hard, close your eyes hard, swallow rapidly, do not upchuck."

I must apologize for not having told you of the other cure I mentioned at the start of this chapter, before, I told you of the penicillin. Anyway, perhaps you'll listen and maybe you'll not. "Remember:" I did promise to show you an Alaska you never dreamed existed.

Old Lady Gunyah, the only name used to identify her, had a sister who was coming to Klawock to pay a last visit, before she died from a huge goiter in her throat. She believed the goiter to be life threatening and more than likely terminal, since it had already been determined that an operation would be too risky.

She spent five months of that summer with her sister, Old Lady Gunyah, before returning Stateside. Upon her return home she noticed that the goiter appeared to be receding, and it kept receding during the remainder of the winter until that time when it became nearly non-existent.

The doctors were somewhat baffled by this turn of events, so immediately launched an investigation in an effort to determine what had brought about this sudden change in their patients condition. After an extensive probe into Old Lady Gunyah's, sister's activities during the past summer, they attributed her cure to the fact that she had been eating seaweed each and every day during her stay in Klawock.

Apparently, the effect of the iodine and natural minerals contained in the seaweed, miraculously affected the cure. At last report the goiter was retrogressing to the point where it was a foregone conclusion the goiter would eventually dissipate, provided that she maintained a daily diet containing an ample amount of seaweed.

Her only comment, "Yes, I eat." "Indian food good."

BEARLY MADE IT

Today's your lucky day fellow travelers, you all get to meet up with a bear, so Join my buddy Frank and I as we comb the forest looking for signs of deer alongside one of the many creeks so prevalent here in S.E. Alaska.

Frank quietly jabbed me in the ribs while at the same time giving me the ssshh sign, as he pointed upwards toward a long ridge of ground on the opposite side of the creek, where he had spotted a brownie. Rest assured, this is not a girl scout I'm talking about, this brownie happens to be a brown bear, and they grow'em big up here. Frank whispered, "If he hears us or get's our scent he'll charge us," "We'd better head for those trees over there."

No sooner than Frank had warned of this the bear raised up on his hind legs, looking at least 12 ft tall. With his nose pointed skyward he proceeded to sniff and test the air around him. "We've got to get up a tree, quick, he's going to come for us." Frank warned. "When they stand on their hind legs like that they're prepared to fight." In our haste to become tree bound we inadvertently created enough noise to allow the brownie to zero in on us, when sure enough, he launched his attack.

What a sight! From our viewpoint in the tree we could actually witness this huge animal literally hurl his body downward, from the ridge above, in an effort to get at us. With legs splayed wide, he actually tobogganed downward over the tops of brush, small trees and rock banks. Everything in his path seemed to bend from his weight as he catapulted down the slope, hitting the creek bed with a tremendous splash amidst a shower of rocks, brush and spray. You have no idea what a resounding racket his actions created. When you stop to realize there were no other sounds to cushion the noise he caused, quite naturally the whole thing was amplified, ten-fold.

Just as I promised, you have just been granted the opportunity to meet up with a bear. However, you must realize as of now, you are no more than ten or twelve feet from him. Ya better be thanking your lucky stars it is, right straight up. Picture yourselves frozen tight against the tree, holding your breaths and not daring to move a muscle as this nasty-assed monster plants his huge 1200 lb. carcass directly below you to begin sniffing and searching you out. From your vantage point (?) directly above the maddened creature, his back appears to be broad enough to carry you and a cousin, both at the same time if you had the notion, which I'm almost positive you sure as Hell do not.

The bear by now, has proceeded to put on a show of power combined with intense rage, as he commences to work himself into a frenzy, systematically tearing up the ground within the immediate area surrounding the tree. The monster is actually foaming at the mouth and shaking his head from side to side, as brush and rocks fly in all directions with the bear seemingly venting his rage at the ground in utter confusion at finding nothing to fight. Fortunately for us, old Mr. mean, after a short period of searching around, finally meandered upstream and out of sight. Frank and I, in your behalf, likewise meandered, only it was downstream, no doubt breaking all existing records for downstream meandering, and we also thanked our lucky stars that we managed to get back to the boat all in one piece.

Of course there was quite a discussion over our encounter with the bear once we were safe aboard the Harry, Jr. Frankie's older brothers readily agreed that we were most fortunate to have located a sizeable tree nearby. They advised us that these big lobo brownies easily tipped the scale at from 1100 to 1300 lbs, and during the mating season, are rated as one of the most aggressive and ferocious animals in S.E. Alaska. They were of the opinion that the elevation we were afforded from being up the tree was enough to prevent ol' Mr. Brownie from locating us through his keen sense of smell, while at the same time it was to our advantage that we had remained motionless while he was throwing a tantrum beneath us. This most assuredly prohibited the ill-tempered monster from locating us through his exceptional sense of hearing.

"I'm thinking, "What the heck, why can't they give a little credit where credit is due. Did we not contribute our share in eliminating the sound factor by exercising great control in keeping our knees from knocking while the bear was stalking us?"

You know, for quite a while following our close encounter with the huge bear, I found myself either singing or humming a song I remembered from childhood. "I think that I shall never see, a poem lovely as a tree."

I've often reflected back on all these startling encounters, and why they came to be, finally realizing the answer to be very simple.

You must learn to accept the fact, the land belongs to the bear, the wolf and the deer, just as the forests belong to the Raven and the Eagle. Then too, one must grant that the seas belong to the whale, the seal and other aquatic life, which surely must include all sea birds, as well.

With due respect to the Brownie or the Wolf. If it is edible, quite naturally he seeks it. In the event something has invaded his privacy, kick it to Hell out'a there. If it is available for loving, fight for it. It's all just as simple as that.

We must learn to accept the fact that we are the intruders. It is we who created the conflict and got what we asked for, thank you. It is true that Alaska has gone through a great amount of change through the advent of time.

YA WANNA PLAY TUG-A-WAR

As I go about unveiling those series of events I've shared with my Indian buddies, Bill, Leo and Frank woods, I'm afraid I've inadvertently failed to give them the credit they rightfully deserve. I would like to impress upon you, dear reader, these guys were the very best woodsmen and hunters one could hope to be associated with. Therefore, I say thank you again, and again, Bill, Leo and Frank for taking me in as a Cheechako, then teaching me the prowess that I too should come to love Alaska and everything about it, as you do. So with no further delay, let us go forth a bit more with my learning process. Today is another of those, "Another, days," and I wonder what this one could possibly have in store for me as I toss my bedroll aboard the Harry, Jr. in preparation for a Halibut trip. As usual, it is early morning with daylight almost upon us. We must time our activities in concordance with the tide which shall be at low ebb before another hour has passed, an ideal condition for capturing a few octopus before setting out halibut skates in Esquibal Channel.

It was just yesterday when the boys requested that I make up a rather special tool made from a piece of round rod 5/16" in diameter, and no less than 16 ft in length. I was further instructed to make sure it had a sharp reverse bend at one end, looking somewhat the same as though I was crooking my finger at someone while saying, "Come over here." I was further ordered to simply bend the other end of the rod at a right angle, like 10", to form a ready made handle that would suffice as a means for tugging. "Hmmm," I wondered, "What's with this tugging bit?" I do have the rod as we pile aboard the boat, heading for a shallow Inlet that has a sandy bottom, where the boys are certain we will encounter octopus. Contrary to our recent clamming expedition, this time we were all required to wear hip boots.

Upon reaching our destination we continued inching forward towards the beach with the power skiff at which time the water became quite shallow, but at the same time afforded us the opportunity to see bottom more readily. After determining we were at the proper depth, we were commanded to toss out the anchors and make fast the skiff, as we all bailed out into water that was just short of hip boot deep. I was amazed at the clarity of the water as we waded shoreward a bit at a time until Frank suddenly stopped short to point at a small mound of sand beside a large rock. "There's one right there Johnnie." Frank had detected a sign that there were octopus inhabiting the area. I had no idea what sign he detected, but I was reasonably sure it wasn't a street sign. Quite naturally I kept this bit of humor to myself for fear they would be of the opinion that I wasn't knowledgeable when it came to spotting octopus sign.

Frank continued, "Now take the rod you bringded and slide it under the rock, but be sure the hook part is pointed straight up. The octopus sleeps upside down under the rocks by daytime. You can tell he's there cause he blew the sand out from the rock to make his den." I peered down through the water and it was just as he had said. There was a small mound of sand beside the rock, which I would never in the world have seen, nor would I have given it any substance, save for these three brothers teaching me their ways.

I was coaxed into shoving the rod far under the rock with the hook end facing up. I was then instructed to yank back hard, hooking the octopus. This I did, and at that moment I was initiated into a tug of war to end all tugs of war. I commenced to pull backwards for all I was worth, while at the same time the damn octopus was hanging on for all it was worth. "Holy yumped up Yimminy," I'm thinking, "The only hunting I was accustomed to doing was maybe hunting down an address in the city, and here I am out in the middle of nowhere doing hand to hand combat with an enraged octopus." Meanwhile Frank is urging me not to give up, "Tug hard, don't slack off, pull, pull, pull!" All at once there was a noticeable sign the octopus was weakening as I gained a half step back. Following this, the octopus released his hold on the rock entirely and I had him.

"Yikes, who has who?" The ugly creature by now has his tentacles wrapped tightly around my leg, and I'm visualizing the monstrous one I saw in the movies, where it grabbed a boat and smashed it. Frankie insistently, once more jarred me back into action, shouting, "Head for the beach, don't let him get away." "Damn it anyway can't he see? I'm the one who needs to get away." However, like the great trainee I am, I dutifully headed for the beach with the octopus wrapped around my legs like I had slipped my girdle. I must admit I was a bit unnerved, because I made waves like I had an outboard motor attached to, well you know where. It was quicker than instantly when I hit the beach in a wild dash of spray, salt water, foam and cold sweat.

Frank immediately leaped forth with his knife drawn, then quickly cut the parrot like beak out of the monster, while declaring, "There, he can't hurt you now." I'm actually finding very little consolation in that, because the hideous creature still has his tentacles wrapped round my leg, brrrr, what a terrifying feeling. Surprisingly, and after the initial shock wore off, Frank and I managed to capture several more octopus before the tide changed to drive us out of there. We were pleased to learn Bill and Leo had managed to capture an equal number of these hideous looking cephalopod mollusks.

So now we're headed back to the larger boat to make preparations for going halibut fishing. In view of the fact that octopus meat happens to be the halibut's favorite food, we were well stocked with the ideal bait for our next venture.

The first step in preparing the bait was to rid the tentacles of an outside membrane which was red in color, and tasted so strongly of iodine, even the halibut were know to reject it. After the skinning process had been completed, the meat was cut up into chunks and from this point on, everyone pitched in to do their share in baiting the halibut skate.

("Skate?") Anyone with an ounce of sense should realize that a halibut is incapable of skating. So in order that you may better understand what it is that constitutes a halibut skate, just read on a bit further and I shall try to explain.

A halibut skate is comprised of a long nylon line, where at each end is attached a 50lb anchor. Between the two anchors, fastened securely onto the main line, are a series of large halibut hooks, spaced approximately three feet apart, and liberally baited with the halibuts favorite food, octtopii. These hooks, are called gangents. and in the minds eye would represent feed stations. The entire skate is being held down on the ocean floor by the 50 lb anchors at each end. The reason for the gangents being three ft in length is due to the halibuts feeding habits. They do not strike a lure or bite at the bait. Rather than that, they drift along the ocean's floor to feed in much the same manner as a vacuum cleaner.

We've actually caught a halibut with a whole can of corned beef, a large raw potato, and a piece of a rubber boot in it's digestive chamber. Hey, don't ask me, I can't explain it either, but at least it proves they vacuum.

Let us continue. The gangent presents the cruising vacuum pump with an enticing chunk of octopus meat, since it is suspended at just the proper depth from the ocean floor for the halibut to capitalize on an easy meal. Oh yes, one other thing. In order that we might locate the spot where we dropped the skate in this vast expanse of water, we must make certain to fasten a tag line on each anchor, to which is attached a large fluorescent ball, called a buoy. If it were not for the buoy, when we returned from hunting we would have no idea where we had made the set. (dropped the skate) Surprisingly, in spite of the hugeness of the buoys sitting in the nowhere of the ocean, they appear to be no larger than the head of a match afloat in a swimming pool.

The tide was at high slack when we returned from hunting to haul in the skate. Fortunately, we were well rewarded with a fine catch consisting of five nice halibut, ranging from 80 to 110 lbs apiece. Also included in the catch were three good-sized red snapper, each weighing in the vicinity of 20 lbs each. So as usual we returned to klawock with a load of goodies to share with all. As soon as we came ashore with the halibut it was readied for drying in order to prepare it for future use, but also to prevent it from spoiling. The halibut is first cleaned then filleted, when it is then sliced as thin as possible, but at the same time one must make an endeavor to keep the slices as large as possible. The best means to accomplish this is to obtain the largest butcher knife you can find because that enables you to carve the fillet into broad elongated slices that are referred to as blankets, because of their size.

After cutting blankets, the next procedure is to set up a drying rack, and the best thing for this is to set up a couple of saw horses with two by fours placed crosswise on top. The next step is to locate an area where you will be afforded the most sunshine, and where you will then proceed to lay fish net over the entire structure. One more chore remains, and that is to spread clean white sheets on top of the netting, as this is where the halibut will be distributed for drying.

The halibut blankets must now be sprinkled liberally with canners salt which acts as a mild cure, (a precooking action) after which the blankets are spread evenly upon the sheets where the sun can do it's part in penetrating the fish with a bombardment of both infra-red, and ultra-violet rays. The Indians place a lot of emphasis on making sure that the blankets are ultra thin, otherwise the sun's rays would not penetrate deep enough, which would cause the fish to spoil rather than dry properly.

We have actually never experienced a shortage of help for continually turning the blankets as they were drying, simply because the rewards for those who had volunteered to do this, were well worth their labor. We always treated the volunteers to a red snapper fillet, plus a share of the halibut after it was dried. I can honestly say that dried halibut is one of the tastiest foods I have ever eaten. I wish I could offer you a bite so that you would understand why I say it is such a treat. Hey, I gotta good idea. How about you folks comin on up here this winter, so's I could offer you some.

PAT MY BACK - - I'LL PAT YOURS

Both my wife and I made a token effort to contribute as much of our own culture in behalf of our Indian friends, as they offered theirs to us. We were in our own way, somewhat influential in teaching them things we perhaps took for granted, not book learnin exactly, but more or less instructing them in matters pertaining to the proper procedure in conducting a wedding or getting all gussied up for the senior prom, etc. Things like that. They truly had the desire to do it up right.

They frequently consulted my wife in regards to social conduct, but were equally as determined to familiarize themselves with Roberts Rules of Order, as a guideline in conducting town meetings or their council meetings, as well. In fact, they were offered these instructions by our two, resident Senators, Al Widmark, and Frank Peratrovich. However, we did assist them in becoming accomplished in smaller things such as the proper setting for their table while entertaining guests just like they did, stateside. Trivial contributions perhaps, but nevertheless deeply appreciated by our Thlinget friends.

I do not lay claim to being a psychologist in any sense of the word, but I do believe our bits of advice encouraged many into developing a feeling of social equality, not that it was necessary in our eyes. Just the same we were somewhat instrumental in instilling honesty, integrity, and a feeling for doing for one another by the example that we ourselves, set.

A perfect example of what I am endeavoring to portray, came about one day when one of the elders in our village, whose name was Spencer Williams, was compelled to fly into Ketchkan due to medical problems. Directly below where I lived on the cannery premises, was a good-sized float, which was utilized by a number of the local fishermen who lived near our end of town. Rather than having to leave their boats at the City float, which was much farther from their homes, they instead elected to tie at our float. The one thing that bothered me the most, was the fact that the natives had developed a habit of exacting pay for anything and everything they did.

From my vantage-point above the float I was constantly aware of their comings and goings. It was apparent that their major wintertime activities included pumping the bilges on their boats at frequent intervals, while at the same time making certain their tie down lines were properly secured.

As I had previously mentioned, the old timer, Spencer Williams, had found it necessary that he fly into Ketchican for medical care, so was forced to leave his boat, Klawock #4, unattended for several days. There was no doubt in my mind that every one of the several other boat owners who tied at the float, were well aware of the fact that Spencer inevitably showed up each morning to pump his boat. This was an absolute necessity, because the boat was leaking badly through the packing gland located at the stern, leaving him no recourse other than to pump the bilges on a regular basis.

It was Spencers intention to keep ol' #4 afloat by pumping her daily until that time when the machinist crews arrived in the spring. He would then be afforded the opportunity to have the faulty gland repacked, then voila! #4 would be seaworthy again. Spencer had been gone for only a couple of days when I detected the water line on old #4 looking awfully low in the water. I immediately hurried down onto the float where a couple of the fishermen were engaged in checking out their own boats, tactfully mentioning that I thought

Spencer's boat was sitting awfully low in the water. They readily agreed with me, while at the same time informed me that Spencer had flown into Ketchikan to see the doctor and maybe wouldn't be back for a few more days, then left.

I couldn't imagine. "What in blazes."

It was obvious to me they weren't in the least concerned that Klawock #4 was very near sinking. This really had me puzzled as I set about pumping the boat dry, myself. I continued to perform this little task each morning until that time when Spencer returned home from Ketchikan.

The very morning of his arrival back into town, no sooner had the plane landed when I observed him rushing down onto the float still dressed in his good clothes, undoubtedly expecting to find his boat sunken and sitting on the bottom, poor guy! The following afternoon I heard a knock upon my door and it was he. "Johnnie, they telled me uptown, you the one what pumped the boat. How much I gonna owe you for dis one?" "Nah Dahnah," (meaning, no money) was my reply. "You don't owe me anything Spence, I'll get paid from someone else."

I realized I had him completely baffled by that one! Therefore, I made an effort to explain to him in much the same wording he would use, in the event that it was he, rather than me offering the explanation.

"Spence, this is what we call the Law of Compensation. When I do something good for you, then you will do something good for someone else. Now, someone else does something good for the nother one. Now pretty soon it comes back to me when somebody else does good to me." "This is the Law of Compensation." Everybody do good for each other, then you get paid with a good feeling, and you have many friends, okay? I'm certain he left the house somewhat confused. However, I learned later that he had carried the message and explained to the best of his abilities, the Law of Compensation, for the benefit of his Thlinget buddies. Shortly thereafter, I detected a slight change in their attitude towards one another, leading me to believe I had made a slight step in the right direction. I'm pleased to relate that it actually got better and better as time went on. They gradually became aware of cooperation and what affect it could effect for one another, a little something they had been overlooking in the past.

Spencer accosted me on the street one morning, requesting a bit more information concerning the Law of Compensation. I impressed upon him, this was not a real law, but one that people make for themselves so that they all may live together in a better way. "Spencer," I asked him. "Remember when I welded Tommy Peratrovich's trike for him?" "Remember when I built the tank stoves in the blacksmith shop for Isaak Kataase, Thompson Peratrovich and Francis, you saw me do those ones. I said Nah Dahnah for them, too! Wahsaw? One time Francis brought me some nice deer meat. Isaak Kataase brought me a nice chunk of halibut. They shared seaweed with me. That is compensation, just like Konash Chees, (thank you) but no money. Now they are my friend, much better than money. This is the part of compensation I like the most."

"Clang," comprehension rang his bell loud and clear, because just a few days later he arrived at my door to present me with a beautifully hand carved, Indian Halibut Hook. Better still, along with the gift, he rewarded me with a broad grin and a warm handshake. I knew for sure he now understood the Law of Compensation, and it worked for me as well, because Spencer became my very good friend. My teachings had apparently taken hold within the rest of the town, because from time to time I was able to witness several acts of cooperation amongst others. However, the greatest proof of all came about one morning when I actually witnessed one of the fishermen pumping another's boat, even though the owner himself wasn't present. I was sure tickled with that one, because only through the power of suggestion could anyone ever dream of coaxing an Indian into changing his way of thinking.

DUK DUUK – THE NORTH WIND

In the town of Klawock there is a small park sitting atop a hill overlooking the surrounding countryside. The park contains a collection of totem poles: each fashioned for a specific purpose. It might be to maintain a record of ancient beliefs, or even the history of one particular family, but more often than not depicts legends relating to the daily lives of the Thlinget nation.

I had just passed through Totem Park on my way to the clinic, which was maintained by the interdenominational missions for Christ, under the auspices of Dr. Lynn McKlenny, the resident physician. When crossing the park I chanced upon George Charles, an old and very knowledgeable Thlinget elder. Quite naturally we struck up a conversation regarding the totems in the park and their significance in relationship to the tribe. How fortunate for me that through George I was able to gather some real genuine and authentic information concerning the totems. From our chance meeting he proceeded to enlighten me as to the true significance of many of the totems, especially those that were severely misconstrued due to the inaccuracy of many who had already been misinformed.

I wondered that a few of the totems were noticeably flat on the backside, while the majority of them were not. George explained this to me in a somewhat fractured use of the Kings English, which was a common occurrence for the elder Thlingets who were not exactly fluid in our tongue. Since it is typical of the manner in which the older Thlingets accented their conversations, I'm going to tangle it up in much the same manner as they conversed with me. In so doing, I'm offering you the opportunity to appreciate how interestingly different it sounded as George talked to me.

"Those flat ones on the back, Johnnie," he explained, while pointing here and there. "Sometimes means the big ones is in there. "They used to put in the bodies of the big ones, then seal up everything with the pitch. Like Chief Takhoma, he was a big one." "Now, some of dis ones," he claimed, as he pointed his finger to single out others, "means the greatness of the family, cause they wanted to be remembered and they make up the totems, heself." He continued to identify others also, that told stories of long ago.

"Look from dis ones right here, Johnnie, they the ones tell about the winds. Dis one, Nanah Khayt, the West wind what brings the snow what eats itself." (I am certain he was referring to a snow squall, followed by a balmy ocean breeze that caused the snow to dissipate in a very short time following its being deposited upon the ground.) Surely we must all have seen this happen at one time or another. George continued to point out the various totems representing individual winds while describing them to me. He noted the East Wind. "Dis the one says the oooh, oooh, oooh noise." Then, "Aha!" he exclaimed excitedly, while he no doubt recalled a story told to him a long while ago. "The North Wind, dis the strong wind, I gonna tell you for this one."

"First he is a cripple boy, Johnnie. He doesn't have any name cause nobody wants to own him. The other boys don't wants to play with him for shooting arrows or for to rassle with them. They tell him, Go play with the girls, but the girls didn't wanted him too. Then he goes to the woods feeling sad. He is alone. Then he eats some herbs and sometimes a squirrel, and bird's eggs what keeps him alive."

"One day the North Wind come to him to be his friend, and tells him. "I will make you strong again if you will like that?" The cripple boy is so happy to have a friend, he says yes for the North Wind to make hlm well. The next day the North Wind came back and throw him down hard. Then he come again and again, to throw him down. The wind tell him. "You must learn to throw me down. You will be the "Strongest Man" if you can do this. He fight against the North Wind many times in the forest, and study hard what makes the North Wind can knock him down, till one day the Raven flew over to him to give him a strong sign, so he threw the North Wind down. Dis make the North Wind howl like he got happy; cause now he knows he will have an adopted son who will be the "Strongest Man."

"Next time, the North Wind came back again to tell him, "You got to keep trying until you can twist the limb out from that big spruce tree, right there, then you must put it back again." Now he is gone! The boy who was a crippled one is now a powerful man, but he doesn't even know it yet, cause he didn't seen anyone for a long time. Instead he worked hard every day to twist out the limb until the Raven flew by. Then it dropped the leaf it was carrying in he's mouth right by him, and he knew right away, the Raven was trying to tell him something. This time he picked up the leaf but instead it was a special herb, so he ate it down. The next day he tried harder to twist out the limb, then all of a sudden it came out, then he twist it back and it stayed."

"The North Wind came roaring in happy, and telled him he was now his son, and was now to have his name, "Duk Duuk," which means "The Strongest Man."

At this point it was rather interesting to notice the transition in George as he changed from merely telling the story to actually living it as his gesturing and enthusiasm increased proportionately.

George continued. "Duk Duuk now knows he is the strongest man and is very happy, cause now he has a father and bear his name, so he's gone back to the village, but everything is bad. A evil spirit, the huge Sea Lion is destroying the next village from them. All the men from his village are climbing into the war canoes that hold seventeen men, to fight the evil sea lion before it comes to destroy his village next. Duk Duuk is eager to go with them, but they tell him, "No, you are not a warrior like us, you stay with the women," but Duk Duuk does not listen this time. He reached out with only one hand to pulled the great canoe with all it's rowers back till he got in too. They didn't even noticed this cause Duk Duuk climbed in the back of the boat. Now, when they camed to the place where the evil spirit was they could see how big he was cause he's an evil spirit, that's how he could got so big."

"They could see the monster knocking down all the tents with he's tail while he was scattering all their food for the winter around, like the fish drying, and the sea lion was eating all of it down. The deer meat with the skins got scattered all around. All the fighters charged out from the canoes with their spears and arrows, but the mean sea lion flipped them everywhere with he's tail. He even killed some of the people already. They didn't notice Duk Duuk until he ran up to the sea lion to grab him by he's tail to make he's nose touched the ground, then he ripped him in two to saved the village."

"This is why they call the North Wind, Duk Duuk," George continued, as he pointed to a totem pole representing Duk Duuk in the act of destroying the sea lion with his bare hands. The totem stands nearly 30 feet tall and is explicit in it's portrayal of a powerful Thlinget warrior standing erect with a huge sea lion locked firmly in his grasp as he tears it asunder, and therefore saves his village from destruction.

George and I stood gazing at the totem for a short period of time, trying to envision such an event taking place, then returned to reality as I bid him, "Konas Chees, George." He gave me a big grin that I had used the Thlinget term for thank you, then turned, heading home, but no doubt reliving the Legend in his mind's eye, again and again.

LEGEND OF THE EAST WIND

In addition to and besides hunting and fishing, there were plenty of social activities right here in the very heart of Klawock that were quite different in comparison to the way we conducted ourselves Stateside. When we lived in the big cities we rarely knew our neighbors, but here in klawock which was a very small village, everyone's life seemed to border on one another's. It worked parallel with and comparable to the old adage, "Birds of a feather."

Because of this, we became close friends with Art Demmert and his wife Virginia, with whom we played cards quite frequently. Of an evening, if we were not at their house, they would more than likely be at ours. Sukway, Arts mother, and Papa George, the father, were very influential in matters pertaining to the Thinget culture, and since we reflected such a close relationship with their son and daughter-in-law, they decided to adopt us into the Thlinget Nation.

My adopted name was to be Kinduh Kut Neek, a name taken from a constellation in the sky, denoting that I was to be regarded as a prince related to the Dog Salmon, one of their prime sources for food. Therefore I was to be held in high esteem as a provider. My wife's adopted name was to be Kuh Kudah Khoon, (I am not really too sure of the spelling), but it supposedly refers to the East Wind. Herein, lies the legend of a small Indian girl who unfortunately was born a cripple, so in the eyes of the Indian was socially unacceptable. Because of this she became an outcast from the tribe. None of the other children would have anything to do with her, so she devised her own means for entertainment by becoming a child of the forest. She became familiar with the deer and their fawns, adopted some baby squirrels, and enjoyed having birds flock around her when she fed them a variety of seeds from the plants she was familiar with. Also, because of her continually inhabiting the forest she became worldly wise in identifying herbs and natural foods offered her by the great spirit of the forest.

One day she happened upon an earthworm that had been trampled by some woodland creature unknown to her. She felt great compassion for the poor thing so she decided to nurse it back to health through her gifted knowledge of herbs and nutritional plant life. Within a very short time she achieved startling results. The earthworm had grown to unimaginable proportions which induced the little crippled girl to regard it as her baby.

She even went so far as to wrap her baby in a blanket every evening, crooning and cooing it to sleep each night before she placed it in it's bed lined with soft moss and leaves. She continued to nurture the earthworm with special herbs, as always, until it became so large she was unable to conceal it from the other children when they entered the woods to play. Upon sighting the monstrous earthworm, they ran terrified into the village to report seeing a monster spirit in the forest that was going to harm the cripple.

Immediately following this disclosure, the monster was slain by the tribesmen, causing the poor little crippled girl to grieve over losing her baby until she reached the point of anxiety and hurled herself over a cliff and was killed. The Indians named her Ku kudah khoon, the East Wind. I've heard this same wind lamenting sadly, haven't you, though never cognizant of the fact, that it was Kuh Kudah Khoon you were hearing.

A DOUBLE TRAGEDY

It was getting on toward evening. A couple of my Indian friends, and I were sorta kickin back and yakkin, while listening to all the jargon coming over the short wave band in our radio room, which incidentally, was located on the cannery premises.

It so happened that the fishing season was in full swing at this particular time. Due to the fact that I had a 75 Watt Northern transmitting and receiving set at my disposal, I accepted the responsibility for keeping in touch with our Klawock fleet in the event of an emergency, or for that matter, to simply relay messages back and forth from town. This was all routine stuff until we were suddenly shocked out of our complacency, when the speaker blared out the news that the Ruby Jean, a seine boat that was part of the Klawock fleet, was in trouble. As the transmissions from the Ruby Jean continued to pour in we were able to draw a clear picture of what was happening.

Apparently the Ruby Jean was just around the corner from us, and while attempting a set in the channel between Craig and Klawock, someone of their crew members had become entangled in the seine and had been dragged overboard. As the transmissions continued coming in from the endangered vessel we came to realize that the crew member in trouble was none other than Ed Peratrovich, the skipper, and also the owner of the Ruby Jean. The crew was helpless to do anything, because the seine was purposely constructed in such a manner that it would sink quickly to the bottom due to the fact that the whole lower half of the webbing was threaded with lead weights like a string of pearls. What

187

a heart rending situation for the crew, and what a terrible shock to the town.

Ed Peratrovich, besides being our Mayor, was one jewel of a fellow. He was truly an honest and direct type of person who, while in office, persistently championed for the betterment of his people. Irregardless of which tribal denomination he was associated with, and irregardless of his political beliefs or social standing, our Mayor, Ed Peratrovich was held in the highest esteem by everyone in the village, so consequently was doubly missed by all.

There was also one other tragedy in our little town of Klawock that bears recounting. A tale involving a boat named, "The Shaft Rock." What an appropriate name for a boat that, to my knowledge, managed to sink like a rock not only once but twice. The first incident occurred late one night when the tide was sufficiently high enough for the Shaft Rock and her crew of two, to maneuver into position under a neighboring cannery's holding bins. Without engaging the motor they manually slithered around pilings and braces by sheer hand power alone, so as to end up directly beneath the fish bin directly overhead.

It was their intention to pirate a load of fish by opening the clean out door in the bottom of the bin, allowing for the fish to flow directly into their boat, After loading up they intended to sneak back out, then resell their salmon to the cannery the following morning by creating the pretense that they had been fishing all night. Yep, you guessed it. The door stuck, they got too many fish, and the Shaft Rock sunk like a rock, right there; and yes, you can assume that cleaning up this mess kept them out of circulation for quite a spell.

The Shaft Rock was not a fishing vessel in any sense of the word. It was a stubby little old double-ender that from a distance would be difficult to determine whether it was coming or going. It was hardly any longer than 23 feet, with the hull painted black and the cab sporting a drab unkempt shade of gray. Unless the boat was observed in bright sunlight, you would have no idea it was present, except for one small detail. When running it actually created prop wash, which left a wake, so this was really the only telltale sign that it was around.

Okay, so here we are in the midst of winter at this period in time. The Shaft Rock was intending to make a trip into Craig, a mere six miles down the line for the purpose of hauling a few drums of stove oil back to Klawock. As you probably already know, Klawock was a dry town, while Craig was not, so naturally the four gents on board were considering having a few drinks, ahem! Strictly as a means of keeping warm while the oil drums were being filled at the Standard Oil dock nearby, Dar Smith, proprietor.

Well now the boys had imbibed, the oil drums had been filled, and the Shaft Rock had her bow pointed towards Klawock heading for home. Everything's fine up to this point, BUT! The gents commenced drinking wine and partying raucously, totally ignorant of the fact that the three oil drums sitting on the afterdeck were forcing the stern downward below the normal water line, which was bad, bad, bad.

During the winter months up here in the North Country those boats that sit idle for any length of time, must suffer the affects from being exposed to the drying winds associated with winter's cold breath. Most generally, the drying out of those seams in their hulls which were above the water line created the greatest problem for the boat owners. This is exactly the situation facing the four young Thlingets aboard the Shaft Rock. The caulking, which is nothing more than twisted strands of cotton pounded firmly into the seams of the hull had dried to the extent that it no longer kept the water from infiltrating the hull. Drinking and driving do not mix, and the same holds true when operating a boat. Unbeknownst to the four young revelers aboard the Rock, she was going down by the stern, like a rock.

When the Shaft Rock failed to return to Klawock that night, It generated a feeling of concern. Therefore, the following morning a search group set out to retrace her path back to Craig. Upon receiving information that she had indeed left Craig for Klawock the previous evening, the search party centered their attention more intensely upon the channel leading back to Klawock. It was then that they discovered an oil slick on top of the water, half way between Craig and home. The Shaft Rock had gone down in less than 25 feet of water. Due to the clarity of these Alaskan waters, one could easily peer downward from above and get the whole picture.

An oil drum could be seen lying beside the hull, while another lay on it's side, though it somehow remained in it's original spot on the afterdeck. The skipper of the boat could be observed in a sitting position with his hands engaged in holding the wheel, while another crew member was lying on his side beside the skipper on the floor of the wheelhouse. The other two members of the foursome apparently had attempted to swim ashore, though failing to do so by a matter of just a few yards.

One body was no more than 35 feet from shore, while the other had come oh so close to making it. His body could be seen lying in water no deeper than waist high, had he been capable of standing. In order to recover the two bodies remaining in the boat it was necessary to rig up a grappling hook, but the two who had made it ashore were retrieved simply by placing a pike pole under the arm pit, then unceremoniously hauling them aboard the rescue craft.

Sure a tough way to go, and irregardless of the fact that these young men were not exactly perfect in the eyes of many, to lose four of them all at one time, nevertheless left those of us who cared for them, shocked and saddened.

SAVED BY THE BIRD

In the eyes of the Thlinget nation, the Eagle is all-powerful and majestic. They are the epitome of freedom as they soar gracefully high above the earth. They also represent the Great Spirit for the traveler because of their ability to see long distances which enables them to guide the wanderers directly to their destination.

On the other hand, in the eyes of the Indian, the Raven represents the all knowing and the provider. He is possessed with the power to conquer over evil and, also, is endowed with the ability to guide the Indian through the path of life with wisdom and good fortune. The Raven is forever leading them in the right direction so that they may surpass any and all obstacles in their path.

Legend has it that many, many years ago the Thlingets were a poverty-stricken clan, since they had just moved into the area and had consumed all the edible plants within their grasp, and here it is that winter is coming on, and the plants will soon be gone. As the Shaman prayed for help for his people the Raven appeared from the sky. He learned of the peoples suffering so he went to the ocean and picked up an octopus. He hovered over the ocean with the octopus held tight in he's beak, making sure that it's tentacles dangled in the water until the octopus had caught a number of fish. He then returned to the tent sights, where there was a stream nearby. He then proceeded to release a number of trout, along with some salmon in the stream, where they propagated and multiplied. That is why, to this very day the Raven is held in reverence for saving the Thlinget nation from starvation, while also providing them with an everlasting food supply, easily supplemented with berries and other edible plant life.

There is a never ending, ending in sharing with you these many years I spent in this amazingly, fabulous land called Alaska.

Nevertheless, I have reached the point where I feel secure in assuming you've all experienced change and adventure and have come to know this mystic and beautiful land a little more clearly after having accompanied me on this journey to "AN ALASKA THAT USED TO WAS." So, it's farewell and may we meet again time, from me to you. (Adios!)

CPSIA information can be obtained at www.ICGtesting.com
Printed in the USA
LVOW01s1806281213

367247LV00019B/1059/A